Altar Prayers

FOR THE CHURCH YEAR

Altar Prayers

FOR THE CHURCH YEAR

CLEMENS H. ZEIDLER

AUGSBURG PUBLISHING HOUSE
MINNEAPOLIS, MINNESOTA

CONTENTS

FOREWORD

The literature of prayer in the church is vast and inclusive. This volume is a small contribution to that sacred body of material and is submitted for the interest of pastors, who may wish to use these altar prayers in their worship services. By the nature of its organization, this book is intended primarily for liturgical churches, following as they do the historic, ecumenical church year. However, pastors of non-liturgical churches may also find it useful as a source for what is called "the pulpit prayer."

The "altar," "general," or "church prayer" of the congregation is one, usually, of such breadth as to incorporate both the timeless needs of the church universal and the equally perennial wants of "all sorts and conditions of men." It is comparable to the Litany. It is essentially a prayer of the people of God, as this people finds *locus* in a specific congregation of the church. The minister is only the spokesman; it is the people of God who pray here. The purely personal note is subdued in favor of the collective voice and cry of God's family. Can there be a more acceptable kind of prayer to our Father than this?

What this book ventures to do, however, first of all, is to provide for Lutheran and possibly other liturgical churches that use the ancient pericopes a series of alternate altar prayers for all the Sundays and chief festivals of the church year. Secondly, it offers prayers related deeply in theme, biblical forms of thought, and content to the particular propers appointed for that day.

If the propers provide the liturgical churches with a systematic, spiritually edifying, and pedagogically sound plan of presenting in a full church year the great essentials of scriptural truth, and interrelate the Introit, Collect, Epistle, Gradual, and Gospel assigned for each service to one or a few dominant notes, it was felt that the general or altar prayer could and should be included in this scheme of things.

The advantage seems fairly clear. Certainly this could be a contribution to the "wholeness" of the worship for that service. It would give a more complete harmony and unity to the service as it gathers in the great supplication of God's people the themes, thoughts, and precepts suggested by the propers for that day.

There may be, moreover, certain pastoral help in this volume. It offers the minister what is hoped are good general prayers when he may feel the need to introduce variety in order to make the general prayer more meaningful.

With these few words of explanation, and with hope that the prayers herein may in their use find their way, like Cornelius', to the throne of God, this volume is committed to the church's worship.

C. H. ZEIDLER

ADVENT

first sunday

Almighty God, Father of all mercies and God of all comfort, who, since the world began, didst give through thy holy prophets the promise of mercy and deliverance, we thank and praise thee for the coming of thy Son Jesus Christ, the Light to lighten the Gentiles and the glory of thy people Israel.

We beseech thee, O God, that as thy faithful people in every age have earnestly and heartily believed thy Word, so we may also unwaveringly believe and be found worthy to obtain thy heavenly promises. And as thy servants in the Israel of the Old Covenant looked with fervent longing for the coming of the Messiah, the Deliverer, grant that we may eagerly and joyfully welcome him, Jesus our Lord, into our hearts by faith, and thus be delivered by his might from the power of sin, death, and the devil.

To this end, dear God, lead us by thy Spirit to an understanding of our great sinfulness and our need of repentance. Teach us to repent. Help us to hate evil and to love the good. Strengthen us against the temptations of all our adversaries. Incline our hearts to seek righteousness and holiness, that thus we may serve and glorify thee.

Send out thy light to all corners of the earth, that men everywhere may know thy love in the gift of thy Son Jesus Christ, and join the multitude of thy people who say, Blessed is he that cometh in the Name of the Lord; hosanna in the highest. Grant peace and tranquility to the nations of the earth. Especially do we ask thy favor upon our own land and all who dwell here. Guide all who are in authority over us, that in all things they may do thy will and acknowledge thee the only true God.

Bless all who are gathered here in thy house this day and sanctify them by thy Word. To those among us who are afflicted in any way, to those who are in sorrow, to those who are enduring trials, to those who may be in any necessity of body or spirit, grant such strength, comfort, and understanding that they, loving thee above all else, may in patience and constancy know the joy of thy abiding presence.

All these things we ask in the Name of him who came for our deliverance, died for our salvation, rose again for our justification, and ever lives to intercede for us before the Majesty on High, even Jesus Christ, our Lord. Amen.

second sunday

O Lord God, the Father of all light and wisdom, who art righteous in all thy ways and true in all thy judgments, we give thanks unto thee for thy Word, for thy statutes and testimonies, for thy laws and commandments, for thy sacred ordinances and thy sure word of prophecy, and most especially for the Gospel of our Lord Jesus Christ. For thy whole counsel we praise thee. We confess with thanksgiving that thy truth is pure, enlightening the eyes; perfect, converting the soul; sure, making wise the simple; right, rejoicing the heart; true, guiding the lost; good, strengthening the weak; and light, leading us to Christ. We ask thy blessing on all who preach, teach, read, and study thy Word, that all men may hear the joyful sound of the Gospel.

O God, fill us with all joy and peace in believing, that we may abound in hope through the power of the Holy Spirit. Help us that we may serve and love thee with pure hearts, worship thee with clean hands, obey thee with willing minds, trust thee with perfect confidence, fear thee and none other, and love thee above all the world. Stir up our hearts, O Lord, to the end that we, trusting in thy Word and promise which have been confirmed unto us by the gift of thy Son Jesus Christ, may here and in the world to come glorify and praise thee evermore.

To this end guard and preserve us that the devil, the world, and our own flesh may not deceive us, nor lead us into error, unbelief, and sin. Teach us to watch and pray always that, abiding faithful even unto death, we may be accounted worthy to escape those things that shall come to pass on the earth and to stand before the Son of man, Jesus our Lord, who shall come to be our Judge. Keep us steadfast in faith and love, that we may in no wise fail to obtain that inheritance which he has promised to all who love and serve him.

We pray for thy church, O God, that all schisms, scandals, and heresies may be put out of the way, and that it may serve thee in truth, purity, and single-minded devotion.

Give peace and stability to the nations of the earth. Put down all evil rulers, and raise up those who will serve after thy good pleasure.

We pray thy blessing upon our homes and families; may Jesus Christ rule in the hearts of parents and children. Give strength and healing, after thy good counsel, to the sick; give comfort to those who sorrow; give guidance to our youth; give joy and hope to the aged; give courage to the perplexed; and lead all of us to look now and always unto Jesus, the Author and Finisher of our faith, who in his Second Advent will receive us and all who believe in him unto himself and unto thee, O Father, and the Holy Spirit. In his holy Name we pray these things. Amen.

thiro sunday

O God, thou Shepherd of Israel, who didst lead Joseph like a flock through all the long years of promise, nourishing and sustaining thy people in the hope of deliverance by the word of thy prophets, and who in the fullness of time didst raise up a Horn of Salvation in the house of David, even thy Son Jesus Christ, grant unto us such a vivid faith in thy promises that we may rejoice and give thanks evermore.

Now, O Father, in this most sacred hour we, thy children, bring thee our prayers and supplications with thanksgiving. According to the necessities of each, send such deliverance as will renew us in body and soul. Forgive our sins and blot out all our iniquities. If any be blind in heart and spirit, open his eyes; if any walk uncertainly, guide him in the pathways of righteousness; if any be impure in thought, word, or deed, cleanse him by thy Spirit; if any be deaf to thy Spirit, open his ears to thy truth, that hearing he may believe and be saved; and if he be dead to the things that pertain to his salvation, quicken him by thy mighty power. Let thy Holy Spirit descend upon us, we pray, that we may not fail in that day when our Lord will come again to bring to light the hidden things of darkness and make manifest the counsels of the heart.

We pray for thy church everywhere throughout the world. Grant thy blessing to all thy servants who proclaim thy Word to the multitudes. Give aid and strength to all missionaries and through them accompany thy Word with power, that all men may know thee to be the only true God and Savior of men. Rule over the hearts of all men, guide the decisions of those in authority, and sit in the secret councils of nations, to the end that peace and justice may prevail. Help all men to know and believe the doctrine of him whom thou didst send, and grant that they may learn that only those things are good, true, and enduring which are in obedience to thy Son Jesus Christ.

Bless all who are gathered before thee this day in the fellowship of the Spirit, especially those here in this thy house. Be with those of our number who are sick or under any affliction of body, mind, or spirit. Comfort them that they may, through their trials, learn of thy gracious power and readiness to help in every time of need. Endow us all with grace, that we may daily show forth the light of thy Name, and the divine excellencies of the Savior of the world, Jesus Christ our Lord.

All these things, and whatever else thou seest we need, we beseech of thee in his Name. Amen.

ADVENT

fourth sunday

O heavenly Father, who hast made all things in heaven and earth to serve thy will and to witness to thy glory and goodness, we give thee our humble and joyful thanks for the coming of our Lord Jesus Christ, and for the salvation thou hast provided for all men in him.

With contrite hearts we turn to thee, O God. We acknowledge our transgressions and confess that we have failed to do the good which we ought to have done, and that we have done the evil which we ought not to have done. Forgive us, and stir us to a quickened sense of our iniquity and sin; awaken us to our need of daily repentance and renewal, and by thy grace deliver us out of all that besets us and causes us to fall. Cleanse the thoughts of our hearts by the inspiration of thy Holy Spirit. Sanctify the words of our lips by the indwelling of Christ our Lord. Perfect in purity and holiness the works of our hands by obedience to thy Word. Hear, O God. Come, heal and renew us. Grant us the remission of all our sins through our Lord Jesus Christ and his merits, so that forgiven we may have that peace which passes all understanding.

And now, in the assurance that thou art nigh to all who call upon thee in truth, we pray for all men everywhere. Let thy Spirit prevail in every home and school, in every shop and store, and in every kind of labor or industry. Show forth thy honor and glory to the nations of the earth; overthrow all who would hinder the progress of the Gospel of Jesus Christ. Succor all who are persecuted for his Name's sake, and prosper all who love thy truth. Be with the homeless, the fatherless, the comfortless, and help them in their affliction to trust in thee, sending them such deliverance as shall turn their hearts and bring them to a confession of that Name which is above every name, Jesus Christ.

For the wounded in spirit, the sick in mind, the distressed in heart, we pray that thou wouldst make thy face to shine upon them. For all strangers, all travelers, and all who are away from home in any service or calling, we pray and beseech thee to accompany them with thy light and love. For captives and prisoners, for the desolate and forsaken, and for all in peril of life or soul, we implore thy aid and comfort. For the sick and the aged, for those in labor and those in any anguish, for the dying and those who mourn their passing, be thou most gracious; lift up thy countenance upon them and give them the perfect peace of thy holy child Jesus.

In thanks for the gift that no words or tongue can describe, the gift of Jesus Christ our Lord, we pray, O heavenly Father, that this gift may be ours in faith. Grant that our hearts may be a fit dwelling place for thy Son and that we may know the joy of his presence, the blessing of following in his steps, and the glory of that crown which he has promised to all who are his in steadfastness of faith and life. In his Name. Amen.

THE NATIVITY OF OUR LORD

christmas eve

Blessed God and Father, thou Fountain of all wisdom and grace, who hast in ages past promised unto the fathers by the prophets the deliverance of thy people from condemnation, in deepest humility we give thee our thanks and praise for the remembrance of thy covenant and the fulfillment of thy promise in the gift of thy Son Jesus Christ. In spirit we stand in holy awe and reverence before the manger of the Christ Child. The Dayspring from on high has visited us, and who can search out the limits of this mercy? That God, the Son of God, should take our mortal form for mortals' sake, who can examine this mystery? That light and life should be given to those who abide in the darkness of evil, who can know what divine counsels decreed so great a thing for unworthy sinners like us? O God, how unsearchable are thy judgments, and thy ways past finding out. We bow in reverence and wonder.

For the giving of this thy Son most beloved we thank thee, O Father. Yea, we praise, we laud and magnify thee forever. We bless thee for the establishment of thy kingdom here upon this stained and weary earth, even among us who deserve only that thou shouldst hide thy face because of our iniquities.

As we assemble to worship thee and to contemplate the mysteries of the incarnation, wherein the Son of the Most High took upon himself the form of a servant and was made in the likeness of men, grant us a sense of gratitude and joy, that life, hope, and faith may be renewed in each of us, and that each one may find in this Babe of Bethlehem the way of salvation, the remission of sins, the deliverance from every evil power, and the hope of life everlasting.

Grant that the incarnate Savior may rule in the hearts of all men everywhere. Extend the dominion of the Prince of Peace to all the nations of the earth. Give growth in grace and knowledge of the Lord Jesus Christ to thy church, that even as the great snows cover the mountains, the waters fill the ocean chasms, and the clouds cover the vast plains so it may abound in love, joy, and peace, and in faith and every good work. To this end help us, O God, to proclaim the Good News of our Savior's birth in church, in home, in school, in shop, and in market place; use each of us, young and old, according to our talents and abilities. Glory to God in the highest, and peace on earth, good will to men! This we pray in the Name of the Christ Child, Jesus our Lord and King. Amen.

christmas day

O God, the Father of our Lord Jesus Christ, who in eternity didst appoint a time for the sending of thy holy Child Jesus, and didst by thy Spirit overshadow the Virgin, and thus didst send our Savior, as true God begotten of thee from eternity, and true man, born of a woman, accept the thanks of thy grateful people for thy love. We praise thee, we glorify thee, we give thanks to thee for the appearing of thy Son Jesus Christ and for the blessed promise that whosoever believes in him should not perish but have everlasting life. We give thanks for the revelation of thyself in him, that to know him is to know thee, to love him is to love thee, to serve him is to serve thee, and to hear him is to hear thee.

Help each of us to enter into the true joys of this day and to welcome the Savior into our hearts. Implant within us such an understanding of this supreme visitation that in fullness of heart we may give thee continual glory and honor and thanksgiving. Open our hearts to receive in faith him whom thou hast appointed the Lord of life and under whose feet thou hast put all things.

Grant also, O Father, that the whole earth may come to the obedience of the Manger Child and to know him as Wonderful Counsellor, Mighty God, Everlasting Father, Prince of Peace. We pray that men everywhere, from pole to pole and from east to west, may acknowledge Mary's Child as Lord and Savior, the incarnate God. Let the light of this truth reach the hardest of hearts and the most stubborn of wills; let it shatter the wretched idolatries and the brittle ideologies of men; and let it pierce the darkness of all who dwell in the shadow and fear of death.

Grant that the glad tidings of the true Christmas may be borne into each home this day, and that all children and parents may know the greatest gift of all, the Child of Bethlehem. Teach all to subdue pleasure in earthly gifts before the wonder of the heavenly gift of Jesus.

Look with compassion on all who are in any want or need this day. We lift up for thy compassion the lonely and the forsaken, the sick and the troubled, the sorrowing and the dying. Bring to their remembrance with renewed power the comfort of Christmas, the Child who is Immanuel, God with us. Grant them faith that thou art the Deliverer of thy people, their Helper in every necessity, the Health of the sick, and the Hope of the dying. Give them the assurance that in Christ thou art nigh to all who call upon thee.

All this we pray in the Name of Jesus, in whom alone is hope of salvation. Amen.

MARTYR

st. stephen

December 26

Merciful God, heavenly Father, who by thy Son Jesus hast called us to an inheritance incorruptible and full of glory and hast promised us in him the forgiveness of sins and everlasting life, we thank thee for the nourishment of thy Word. Grant through thy Holy Spirit that it may minister to our soul's need and uphold us in all trials and necessities. Especially do we thank thee for the lives of all thy faithful witnesses in every age, who in tribulation and danger trusted in thee, and denied not the faith though the hazards and persecutions were great. Especially do we thank thee this day for the example of thy martyr, St. Stephen, who, when he was reviled, reviled not again, but committed himself to thee, O God, who judgest righteously.

Grant unto us a like spirit in all things, to be filled with faith and the Holy Ghost so that our words and works may be endowed with power. Supply us with grace and wisdom so that through us men may come to know thee and thy Gospel of peace. Fill us with all the fullness of Christ so that we may forgive those who would harm us, and pray for those who would despitefully use us. May we be of such mind and heart that our obedience to thy Word and truth may never falter even in our last hour.

We pray now, O Father in heaven, for all the children of men. Bestow upon them everywhere an understanding of thy love and power, and a spirit of peace and concord. Let thy Name be honored in our homes and in our schools; let thy truth and justice prevail in commerce and court; and let thy righteousness reign throughout the entire fabric of our society. Defend our land from all its enemies and endow those in authority with a right perception of duty and a willingness to perform the same. Save us from all evil, keep us in the faith even unto our end, and receive us at last unto thyself in eternal glory. We ask all these things in the Name of Jesus. Amen.

st. john

December 27

O almighty and everlasting God, who by thy Word hast created and dost uphold all things that are in heaven and on earth, we give thee thanks for the revelation thou hast given of thyself and of thy will and purpose. We praise thee that by thy Spirit holy men were moved to speak and write the things thou didst reveal unto them for our learning and edification, for our warning and comfort, for our reproof, and for our doctrine, so that we might have hope.

We give unto thee our thanks for all thy blessings, but especially for the calling of the holy apostle and evangelist John, and for his witness in word and deed. Help us to continue steadfast in his doctrine that our understanding may be enlightened and our will perfected. Grant that through the writings of the beloved disciple, to whom thou didst grant wondrous visions of thy glory, every thought may be brought into captivity to the obedience of Christ, the incarnate Word, and that we may believe that Jesus is the Christ, the Son of God, and thus possess life through his Name. Inspire us to see and know him as the Word made flesh, the Bread of Life, the Water of Life, the Resurrection and the Life, the Good Shepherd, and the Great High Priest, and to see in him thy love, O Father, who didst give thine only-begotten Son that whosoever believeth in him should not perish but have everlasting life.

For thy people we pray, heavenly Father, even as our Lord did pray, that they may be one even as thou and thy Son are one. Heal all schisms that divide thy church, and bring all into the unity of the Spirit and of faith in accordance with thy will. Grant grace and peace to all lands and nations, and bless all who dwell in our country. Give us rulers who govern in thy fear, and citizens who acknowledge thee in grace and in commandment. We beseech thy most special favor upon the sorrowing and the sick, that thou wouldst deliver them out of all their trials. Comfort the aged, counsel the young, and keep us all within thy watchful care.

These things we ask in the Name of the only Savior of men, Jesus Christ, who is for us now and always the Way, the Truth, and the Life. Amen.

the holy innocents

December 28

O God the Father everlasting, who didst manifest thyself in the flesh in the person of thy Son Jesus, whom thou didst send to a wicked and perverse world, we give thanks to thee for the great love wherewith thou hast loved us and for the redemption thou hast worked for us in thy holy Child Jesus. We, thine unworthy servants, acknowledge our transgressions and we perceive the great wickedness of the world, whose evil is so deep as to take the lives of those children whom we remember before thee this day. Help us to see how great is the evil of this world and to seek after righteousness and all those things which pertain to our salvation.

Heavenly Father, we pray that thou wouldst defend and save thy people everywhere. Most especially do we pray this day for all who are persecuted for thy Name and for thy truth's sake. Bring to naught every evil counsel and purpose which would hinder the hallowing of thy Name and prevent the coming of thy kingdom. By thine almighty wisdom and power overthrow all who hate thy Word and hurt thy people. Break down all who would exalt themselves above thy glory, and who are wise in their own conceit. Let no flesh glory in thy presence. Cast down vain imaginings of human power and grandeur, and pull down the strongholds of that false wisdom which denies honor to thee.

Then, Father of all mercy, grant strength and faith, wisdom and courage, grace and every blessing to those who are oppressed for

Christ's sake. Reveal unto them the deep things of the Spirit to support and sustain them. Give them a full measure of the fullness of Christ. Show them that the foolishness of God is wiser than the wisdom of men; and the weakness of God stronger than the strength of men. Give them the victory which overcomes the world, and the faith that transcends all adversity.

Hear our prayer for all children and grant that in Christ their holy angels may keep them from all harm. Protect them from neglect and from overindulgence, from false teachers and all who would destroy their faith, and bring them all in thine own time into thy everlasting kingdom. All these things we beseech thee in the Name of him, even thy Son Jesus, who in his nativity sanctified all childhood. Amen.

FIRST SUNDAY AFTER

christmas

O Lord God, Father in heaven, who in the fullness of time didst send forth thy Son to be the Light of the world and to gather for thee out of all the kindreds of the earth a redeemed people, we give thee praise and thanksgiving, we bless and hallow thy Name that thou hast so graciously provided for us and for our salvation. We thank thee that through faith in thy Son Jesus Christ we have received the adoption of sons, that we may call thee, in spirit and in truth, Abba, Father, assured that thou art most truly our loving Father and that we are thine own children.

O Father most loving, grant that we who are under the yoke of sin, may in Christ be redeemed and regenerated both in body and soul, and that we may ever be thy obedient servants. Empower us by thy Spirit to perform the works meet for repentance, and faithfully to do thy will with a glad heart and a pure mind.

We beseech thee, dear Father, to show us thy mercy, deliver us from all evil, and rescue us from the due reward of our sins. Shield us in the hour of temptation and make us to will and do only those things that please thee. Grasp us with thy fatherly hand and lead us from the feverish ways of the world to green pastures and still waters. Bestow on us a true faith and a holy love, that the Child whom thou didst send for the great testing of men may be set for our rising rather than our falling.

Heavenly Father, we implore thee to let thy grace rest upon us that we may wax strong in the Spirit, be filled with wisdom, and grow in all that which finds favor in thy sight. Let the brightness of thy glory shine upon all who feel the need of thine almighty aid. Illuminate hearts filled with darkness and homes overshadowed with sorrow or suffering. Give the light of truth to all in authority in our own land and elsewhere, and make all our schools fountains of thy divine light in a world that lies in the shades of strife, superstition, and ignorance.

Establish the reign of the Prince of Peace over the nations of the earth. Visit with thy mercies thy whole creation and every commonwealth of peoples, and, that all may be saved and none lost, bring them to the obedience of that holy Child whom thou didst send for the redemption of all mankind, even thy Son Jesus, the Word made flesh. Let the light of his life: his word, doctrine, and precept; his miracles, signs, and wonders; his birth, ministry, and character; his Passion, death, and resurrection, be that light of divine truth which shall brighten every land.

For our sick, our wounded, our hurt, our troubled, our fallen, and our absent fellow believers we pray. Grant unto them whatsoever they may need: soundness of body, strength of faith, or security of hope; and grant them all in Christ assurance of salvation.

Hear us, O Father, in these our petitions, and direct and govern our hearts that we may be preserved in the one, holy, Christian faith unto everlasting life. Amen.

NEW YEAR'S DAY

the name of jesus

O God, almighty and ever-living Lord, who in thine unsearchable wisdom and infinite grace didst send thy Son in the likeness of sinful flesh and didst make him subject to the Law, that by his perfect obedience and sacrificial suffering he might condemn sin in the flesh, grant unto us the circumcision of the heart so that we may walk, not after the flesh, but after the spirit of our Lord Jesus Christ.

We thank thee, O Father, for the Name which was given thy holy Child, a sign for all ages that thou only art the Source of all redemption and salvation for the multitudes of earth. We praise thee that thou hast set him at thine own right hand in the heavenly places, far above all principality, and power, and might, and dominion, and every name that is named, not only in this world, but also in that which is to come. Help us ever to hallow the Name of Jesus by our obedience to his teaching and example.

We offer thee our thanks, O God, for the blessings of this past year and the divine provision thou didst make for our needs. For family and friends, for home and harvest, for food and raiment, for health of mind and body, for labor and leisure, for law and government, for peace and order, for our preservation in the faith, and for the hallowed times of worship and communion with thee, we thank thee. Forgive us for all things wherein we have sinned. Heal the wounds we have caused in others. Grant us remission for our failures to do what we ought to have done. Deliver us from the evil consequences of our errors, our omissions, our mistakes, and all our transgressions.

And now, O Father in heaven, let thy hand rest in benediction upon this new year, to the end that we may increasingly discover the exceeding riches of thy grace in Christ Jesus, that in sorrow or joy the eyes of our understanding may be enlightened, and that in prosperity or trial we may know the working of thy mighty power and the hope of our calling. Help us that whatsoever we do in word or deed we may do it to thy glory.

Be thou the Shepherd of our youth and the Guardian of all children, the Health of the sick and the Staff of the aged. Grant that in whatever befalls us we may see thy loving hand and, in Christ, possess the sure confidence that all things work together for good to them that love thee. Be thou the Defender of thy people everywhere, and the unfailing Watchman of our own land. Prosper us in the things that make for peace and righteousness, and protect us from every evil. All these things we ask in the one Name whereby we must be saved, Jesus Christ, our Lord. Amen.

SECOND SUNDAY AFTER

christmas

O Lord God, Father in heaven, who in the sending of thy Son Jesus Christ didst in a marvelous manner commend thy love to us and show forth thy great kindness, we thank thee for this unspeakable gift and for the promise that through his Name whosoever believes in him shall receive remission of sins.

We beseech thee to bestow upon us the fullness of his grace, that we may perceive thy glory and truth in him. Help us to receive him into our hearts in faith, so that, believing in him as thy perfect revelation, and trusting him as our only and perfect Savior, we may have power to become thy sons and daughters and heirs according to the hope of eternal life. Grant by thy Holy Spirit that we may be guided by the light of Jesus Christ in all wisdom, counsel, and understanding, that our way may be cleansed, and that we may walk in obedience to his commandments, teachings, and example.

Bless, we pray thee, O God, thy church and thy people and endow them with power and zeal. Strengthen them by casting out all unrighteousness, and by prospering all holiness. Keep the feet of thy saints, that they, rejoicing in thy salvation, may exalt thy Name and show forth thy honor and praise.

Extend thy dominion, O Judge of all the earth, over all lands and nations, and give righteous wisdom to all who rule, so that men may be governed in peace, justice, and mercy. In all homes, give parents grace and wisdom to rear their children in the fear of the

Lord, which is the beginning of all wisdom. In all schools, grant to teachers such knowledge as will direct them to the truth as it is in Christ our Lord. In all hospitals and harbors of the afflicted, give strength and understanding to those who, under thee, help and heal. In all places of industry and commerce, lead men to a clear understanding, that they may serve thee whatever their employment or position.

Be with all who travel, with all in peril of body or soul, with all who are imprisoned, with all who face temptation, and grant to them a sure sense of thy presence.

In these and in all other things in which we stand in need, give, O Father, thy help and mercy. We pray in the Name of thy beloved Son Jesus Christ. Amen.

the epiphany

January 6

Heavenly Father, eternal God, whose alone and forever is the power, and the kingdom, and the glory, and to whom only belongs authority over all the earth and universe, over all forces and energies, over all suns and stars, and over all intelligences and knowledge, we give thee thanksgiving and praise.

We thank thee that by the leading of a star thou didst bring to the feet of our Lord the wise men from the East to manifest thy Light to the Gentiles. Lead the nations of the earth to acknowledge Jesus Christ as Lord, and grant wisdom to all rulers of men, that they may serve him in love and fear. Prosper and bless thy Word and the preaching of the Gospel, that multitudes may come to faith in Jesus Christ and that he may be for salvation unto the ends of the earth. Endue all ministers, missionaries, catechists, and Christian workers with heavenly power and grace, that their labor may be abundantly and fruitfully blessed. Grant all who hear thy Word faith to believe it, strength to obey it, and courage to profess it in word and deed. Give to thy Son the nations for his inheritance and overcome and confound all enemies of his truth. Overthrow all powers of darkness that bind men in the chains of superstition and ignorance, and all forces of denial and unbelief that assault men's minds. Grant help to thy servants who here and in distant lands wage a holy war, until at last every knee shall bow and every tongue proclaim that Christ is Lord to thy glory, O Father.

We beseech thee to behold thy people as they are gathered here before thee. Lead us to bring to thy Son the treasures of our time and talent and likewise yield to his service the whole of our lives, conforming our minds, our wills, and our hearts to his obedience. Grant that we may ever walk in the light which is in Jesus, and that steadfastly following in the path set before us we may at last receive the crown of life.

For our sick we pray that thou wouldst look upon them in mercy and show them the way out of all their trials. Comfort with thy presence the aged, the lonely, and the forsaken. Shepherd the young. Console the sorrowing. Heal the broken-hearted. Forgive us all our sins and grant us newness of life in Jesus Christ, in whose Name we bring these and all our petitions. Amen.

fIRSt sunday

We bless thee, O God, for the revelation of thy will and wisdom in the life of thy Son, Jesus Christ our Lord, even in the days of his early youth.

By thy Holy Spirit implant in us more and more of the mind of Christ. Make us glad to go into thy house. Open our ears that we may gratefully hear and attend to the teaching and preaching of thy Word. In all things, instill in our hearts, O Lord, a continuing desire to be about thy business, to increase in wisdom, and to grow in favor with thee and our fellow men.

By thy mercy, O God, lead our children and young people as thou didst direct and lead thy holy Son Jesus. Give us grace as parents and elders to show thy will and way to the young by faithful worship and love for thy Word and gracious Gospel.

In all our doings, heavenly Father, enable us as young and old alike to present our bodies a living sacrifice, holy and acceptable unto thee. Deliver us from conformity to this world, and transform us by the renewing of our minds, that we may show forth thy good and acceptable and perfect will in our every thought, word, and deed.

Hear our prayer, O God, for all in the company and fellowship of thy church. Prosper and bless our worship and our witness to Christ and his power to save. Fill us more and more with zeal for the salvation of men and the extension of Christ's kingdom. Grant thy strength and blessing to all pastors, teachers, and missionaries, that they may proclaim thy Word with fervor and diligence and bring the light of the Gospel to people of all lands and nations.

Grant, Lord, that by thy Holy Spirit all weaknesses in thy church may be overcome, all lassitude dispelled, all fear of men cast out, all indifference removed, all lukewarmness banished, and all love of the world forsaken. Then by thy same Spirit, fill us all in thy church with a full measure of his power, that we may be obedient to our Lord's commandment to proclaim the Gospel to every creature.

Lord, thou art mighty to save. Thou art the mighty God who spake and it was done, who commanded and it stood fast, who didst order the stars in their courses, the winds in their journeys, the waves in their ebb and flow. Help us to know and find strength in the greatness and wonder of thy might and majesty.

And in thy mercy, Lord, show thy strength and goodness to the sick and the afflicted. Give them grace to cast their cares upon thee in the knowledge and assurance of thy care for them. Help, heal, establish, and strengthen them, and in all things enable them and all of us to rejoice in thy holy Son, our Savior Jesus Christ, whom we worship and adore with thee and the Holy Spirit, one God, world without end. Amen.

EPIPHANY

second sunday

Almighty and ever-living God, who in Jesus Christ thy Son hast given the light of thy truth for all who are in the darkness of error and falsehood, so that all men may have life through his Name, we thank thee that thou hast called us into this true and living faith and graciously bestowed upon us manifold gifts of grace.

Hear now our prayer, heavenly Father, that thy people may be shining lights in this world's darkness. To this end grant that we may be united in brotherly love and zeal to do the holy work set before us, fervent in the purpose of our calling, loyal in every test of faithfulness, joyful in our promised hope, steadfast in every trial, benevolent toward all men, generous in hospitality, and holding fast to all that is good. Grant that we who are called out of darkness into the marvelous light of Christ may thus show forth his praises.

Bestow a special measure of thy grace, O God, upon our homes. As our Lord favored the marriage feast in Cana with his presence and first miracle, and manifested his power and glory amid the scenes of family love, grant that he may be the heavenly Guest in every home and the Guardian of its faith and life. Bless, we pray thee, all who live together in the bonds of holy matrimony, so that in obedience to thy Word they may serve one another in love, hold each other in honor, and acknowledge thy goodness and grace in one spirit even as they are one flesh. Grant that all who enter the holy estate of marriage ordained by thee may do so in reverence, purity, and godly love.

30

Give stability, peace, and tranquility to the nations of the earth, and deliver all people from famine, pestilence, fire, flood, storm, earthquake and every peril, and show thyself the God who alone doeth wonders, so that all men may know of thy power and glory. And send forth ministers of thy Word that the multitudes may learn of thy infinite goodness and love in the gift of thy Son and his Gospel of grace and mercy.

We implore thy mercy, O God, for all who may be in any special want or need of body or soul, that thou wouldst manifest thyself unto them in their deliverance from all evil, giving them the oil of joy for mourning and the garment of praise for heaviness, the light of hope for despair and the song of victory for defeat. Save us from all the hidden perils that surround us, and defend us now and always, even to that hour when thou shalt call us from this earthly tabernacle to dwell in thy house forever and ever. In the Name of Jesus, the Christ, the Son of the living God. Amen.

third sunday

O God, the Father of our Lord Jesus Christ, who among all nations and peoples seekest them that would worship thee in spirit and in truth, we, who are here gathered for thy worship and praise, implore thee that we may be now so inwardly moved in spirit and so filled with thy Word and truth that thou wouldst find acceptable our imperfect sacrifices of thanksgiving, praise, and prayer.

We thank thee, Father, for the sending of thy Son Jesus, and for making known in him the mystery of thy gracious will, that everyone who sees the Son and believes in him may have everlasting life. For our redemption through the blood of his cross, for the forgiveness of our sins, for deliverance from all evil, and for the hope of glory, we give thee thanks. We praise thee that thou hast bestowed upon us thy saving Word, through which thy Holy Spirit has enlightened our understanding and sanctified our wills. We pray, O God, that thy Word may have free course in the lives and hearts of multitudes from east to west, to the end that Christ may reign "where'er the sun doth his successive journeys run," that thy house may be filled with believers out of every kindred and tribe, and that heaven and earth may ring with songs of praise for this great salvation.

Bestow upon us a sure faith in thy power and a perfect trust in thy love, so that we, living out our short span of years in this world, may by applying our hearts unto thy wisdom, and by the exercise of brotherly love, peaceableness, and charity, manifest thy grace, goodness, and glory. Graciously defend us so that we be not overcome of evil; inspire us that we overcome all evil with good. From perils known and unknown, from all hazards to body or soul, against all temptations and trials, preserve us, O Father, so that we may live to serve thee in all godliness and humility.

Watch over thy church throughout the whole world, and grant unto it faithful pastors who are true shepherds and sentinels for thy people.

For all who have the cares of State in their hands, guide them in wisdom and understanding, that they may give effect to thy will, and so govern that all men may eat their bread in quietness and peace.

Graciously help us to redeem the time, using our days wisely toward the upbuilding of faith in our hearts and the hearts of others. Stir up in us such gifts as thou hast bestowed, that these may be used to the spiritual enrichment of our lives. Renew us in the spirit of our minds; turn our footsteps to the pathways of eternal life; cleanse us of all sin; heal us of every disease; comfort all who are afflicted; guard our loved ones wherever they may be; shield us from the powers of wickedness; give us each day our daily bread; and make us contented in whatever condition is appointed to us. As we have received Christ Jesus the Lord, so let us walk in him, rooted and built up in faith, and abounding in all good works. All these things we pray in the Name of him who loved the church and gave himself for it, Jesus Christ, our Redeemer. Amen.

fourth sunday

Almighty God, thou Fountain of all mercies, thou Well-spring of all comfort, who art ever ready to hear the prayers of thy people and hast promised thy saving help in every time of need, as we lift up our hearts unto thee we give thee our humble and heartfelt thanks for all thy gifts and graces.

For the spirit of wisdom and understanding in thy Word and will, for the gift of counsel and might in seasons of adversity, and for the grace of spiritual knowledge and holy fear, we thank thee. But most of all do we thank and praise thee, O Father, for the coming of thy Son and for the promise in him of the life that now is and that which is to come.

Make us mindful of thy desire to save all men in him. Show us the fields white unto the harvest. Open our eyes to the vast multitudes who await the sound of the Gospel. Then open our hearts to an enlarged sense of our responsibility to share the glorious Gospel of our Lord Jesus Christ, and to pray for laborers for the harvest.

To this end, O God, enlighten our minds, that we may know thy will and walk in thy paths. Lead us into all truth, and instill in us charity toward all mankind. Grant us a larger faith in thy mighty power, a deeper trust in thy merciful providence, and a more perfect love of thy Son. Help us to see in him the image of thyself, the revelation of thy grace, the reflection of thy glory, the incarnation of thy

Word, the manifestation of thy presence, and the evidence of thy care for all the children of men.

We pray also for all our homes and families, that thou mayest hallow each one by thy presence. Give them the spirit of Christ, that the children may grow in wisdom and stature, in favor with God and man, that the parents may, by pure love and worthy example, maintain their homes in peace and godliness. Grant that both children and parents may delight to be in thy house and in the true service of thy Son.

Comfort and bless those who are afflicted among us, that they may in love perceive thy good and gracious will and find release from all their trials. Preserve and maintain for us, and for all men, good government, integrity, honest citizenship, and dignity. Put down all who are self-seeking opportunists, purge out all who intend revolution and strife, and suppress those who seek power through the weakness of men.

Keep us and all thy people, heavenly Father, in the unity of the faith and in oneness with Christ through his church. We ask all these things in his Name and for his sake. Amen.

fifth sunday

O Father in heaven, whose we are and whom we serve, thy kingdom come.

We thank thee for the manifestation of Jesus as Lord and Christ, and as King forevermore; and we pray that his dominion may be established from sea to sea, and from the rising to the setting of the sun. We thank thee that thou hast given mankind a divine Sovereign whose law is love, whose crown is truth, and whose scepter is righteousness; and we pray that every nation, kindred, and tribe may confess that he is Lord to thy glory. We give thee thanks that though he is King of kings, yet he was tempted in all points as we are, so that he might be a worthy Savior, able to save all that come unto thee by him.

May thy kingdom come unto the multitudes of the earth. Give the heathen for Christ's inheritance. Cause the kings of the earth to bow before him, and let all the earth see that he only is for the healing of the nations. Bare thy holy arm in the eyes of all lands, and let all the ends of the earth see the salvation of our God.

And as thy kingdom is within us, a spiritual realm of the heart, may thy kingdom come in new power and strength to us also, O Lord. May the peace of Christ rule in our hearts in thankfulness and praise. By his example teach us to trust in thy Word and to be obedient to thy commandments. For his sake give us grace to be merciful and kind, to be humble in mind and lowly in spirit. In his Word show

36

us the pathways to true wisdom. In his sufferings, death, and resurrection grant that we, redeemed in body and soul, may be dead unto sin and alive unto righteousness. And by the inspiration of Christian fellowship in worship lead us to rejoice in thy grace and to give thanks for thy mercy. Grant that thus thy kingdom may come to us.

For thy church on earth we pray, O God. Save it from weakness and error, from unfaithful shepherds and false prophets. Deliver us from heresy and schism. Defend us against the seed of Satan and the terror of godless men. Grant that thy church may be secure against the powers of hell. Teach thy people to be patient in hope, steadfast in faith, and instant in prayer, until the time when thou shalt send forth thy angels to gather thine own into thine everlasting kingdom, and when the righteous shall shine forth as the sun and be joyful forever and ever.

To this end give comfort to those who mourn, patience to the sick, peace to the anxious, strength to the weak, abundance to the needy, and forgiveness to the repentant. Bestow thy mercy on all of us, and teach us ever to set our affection on the things which are above, where Christ our Lord ever reigns to help us. In his most holy, precious, and glorious Name we pray. Amen.

the transfiguration

Almighty God, whose eyes are upon the righteous and whose ears are open to their prayers, hear now the prayer of thy people and grant us all such things as we need for the health of our souls and bodies.

We praise thee, O God, for the precious gift of thy Son. And we bless thee especially this day for the revelation of thy will in our Savior's glorious transfiguration on the holy mount. By this mighty sign give to us, Lord, and to all thy people a clearer vision and higher knowledge of Christ. Give us grace to behold him with the eyes of faith in the splendor of his eternal deity and to worship and adore him in sincerity and truth. And grant that as we behold the radiance of his heavenly beauty, we may know him and believe in him as the Light of the World, the Sun of Righteousness, and the express image of thine own divine Being.

By the sign of thy voice and command, Lord God, give us quickened faith in the doctrine of thy Son, a joyful readiness to believe his promise, and a spirited willingness to heed his commandments. By the sign of the bright cloud manifest to us each day the radiant presence of thy holy angels, and assure us of their charge concerning us. And in the sign of Moses and Elijah show us that blessed are the dead who die in faith, blessed are they who live in Christ, blessed are all who believe, for they shall know the power of his resurrection and shall be "changed from glory into glory."

O God and Father, as thou didst in Jesus make humanity the shrine of thy Godhead, let thy Holy Spirit find a tabernacle in our poor bodies and transform our weak, sinful lives into the radiance of goodness, purity, and righteousness. Transform our minds by the renewing grace that flows from thee. Transform our vision, our understanding, our judgments, yea, our whole persons, to reflect the mind of Christ. Take our sicknesses, pains, wounds, and hurts; take our disappointments, defeats, and despair; take our sorrows and mourning; take our pride and anger; take our selfishness and envy; take our hate and fear; take all these, O Father, and transform them by the touch of Jesus into noble impulses, pure motives, kind thoughts, constructive deeds, high courage, and true faith.

Look upon thy church, O Lord, here and in all places, and grant that we and all who bear the Name of Christ may daily offer up to thee the acceptable sacrifices of repentance, thanksgiving, and loving obedience.

Behold our nation, O God. Deliver it from all workers of iniquity and purge it from all unrighteousness. Have mercy upon us, and by thy great power save and defend us.

For our whole world we pray. Grant that thy way may be known upon earth, thy saving help among all nations.

Thou who art nigh unto all them that call upon thee in truth, hear our prayer and by thy mercy grant our petitions for Christ's sake. Amen.

septuagesima sunday

O God, heavenly Father, who art our Rock and our Fortress, our Joy and our Salvation, our Light and our Life, our Sun and our Shield; and who art plenteous in mercy toward all them that call upon thee, we give thee thanks and praise.

We thank thee that thou hast called us to faith in Jesus Christ, our Redeemer, made us citizens in his eternal kingdom, clothed us with the armor of righteousness, and given us the spirit of power, of love, and of a sound mind. Preserve us therein. Fill us with the fruits of righteousness. Make us living epistles of thy Son Jesus Christ.

We thank thee that thou hast called us to be laborers in thy vineyard, and hast assured us that our labor for thee is not in vain. Grant that our work for the salvation of souls and the advancement of thy church may be acceptable in thy sight. Give us willingness, diligence, obedience. Give us good heart to accept every service, wisdom to perform it well, and the mind to do it faithfully. Give us gladness for all who come soon or late to join us in the labors of thy church. Give us grace to welcome them as brothers in Christ and co-heirs of his salvation. Give us patience and strength to bear the burden and heat of the day. Keep us under thy providence and care, and as we pass through this world's sea of trials and tribulations, may we find true refreshment at the Fountain of life and truth which is Jesus Christ.

We pray, O God, that we may be ever mindful that the church is the body of Christ and that he is its only head. Help us, then, in all testing, in all temptation, and in all trial to be loyal to him, steadfast in faith, and to acquit ourselves as true soldiers of the cross. In every opportunity to advance the borders of his kingdom, lead us forward to possess the land. Aid us to lay hold of every challenge to rise to newness of life, so that we, thy people, may not be conformed to this world, but be transformed by the power of the Gospel. Give us the mind of Christ. Let none of us glory in his own wisdom, or power, or riches, but only in this, that he may know and receive of thy wisdom, power, and riches in the life, the death, and the resurrection of thy Son Jesus.

Be with us, O God, in all that we do; in our daily toil, strengthen and counsel us; in our leisure, defend us; in our homes, shelter us; in our travels, guide us; in our study, counsel us; in our afflictions, shield us; in our sorrows, comfort us; in our prayers, hear us; and in our worship, lift up our souls to thee. May we run the race that is set before us with faith and courage so that we may obtain the crown of life.

Accept now the sacrifices of broken spirits and contrite hearts, and grant unto us thy grace and truth in the saving knowledge of our Redeemer, Jesus Christ, in whose Name we pray all these things. Amen.

SexaGesima Sunday

O Lord God, who art gracious and full of compassion, slow to anger and of great mercy; who art good to all and whose tender mercies are over all thy works, fulfill now the desire of them that call upon thee, and hear the secret prayer that rises in each heart.

In thankfulness and humility we bow in spirit before thee, O God, for commending thy love to us in the death of thine only-begotten Son, who was delivered for our offenses and raised again for our justification. We acknowledge before thee our transgressions; our sin is ever before us. Grant us a true understanding of the character of our sinfulness and our need of repentance. Show us that, in Christ, if we will confess our sins, thou art faithful and just to forgive us our sins and to cleanse us from all unrighteousness.

Bestow upon us the gifts of thy Holy Spirit, that as thou dost sow the seed of thy Word in us, we may receive it in honest and good hearts and, having heard it, keep it and bring forth fruit with patience.

Save and defend thy church from evil, and grant unto all who serve thee in thy church faithfulness to thy truth, diligence in labors, patience in sufferings, and the blessed hope of eternal life. Especially do we ask thy aid upon all missionaries in distant lands, that their work may be prospered in the harvest of souls. Guard them by thy power from all perils of body or soul.

Let thy light shine in every institution of the church, in schools, in hospitals, and in homes for the burdened and afflicted, and grant unto them thy favor, that in all things those who serve and those who are served may taste of thy goodness and grace.

For our government we pray. Give us, O God, unselfish governors and trustworthy magistrates, honorable legislators, a law-abiding citizenry, a public education that will aid the church in the development of Christian character, and a society that will mirror all goodness and virtue.

Bless our homes and make them the dwelling places of thy Spirit where Christ is honored in the teaching and love of the parents and in the obedience of their children.

We beseech thy mercy upon our sick. Help them to know the power of Christ, that they may glory in their infirmities. Set divine healing forces to work in their lives and cause them to find the joy of thy salvation. Comfort the sorrowing; be with the lonely; strengthen the aged; and to any who are in great perplexity or anxiety, temptation or trial, give faith in thy power and mercy, and lead them to see that the grace of Christ is sufficient for any adversity.

Let the word of Christ, then, dwell in us richly in all wisdom, and help us to receive the end of our faith, even the salvation of our souls. In the Name and for the sake of Jesus our Savior. Amen.

quinquagesima sunday

O Lord God, whose ways are mercy and truth to such as keep thy covenant and thy testimonies, let thy peace, like the gentle dew from heaven, fall upon all who have come this day into thy house to offer unto thee the sacrifices of praise and thanksgiving.

For thy Name's sake pardon our iniquity. Remember not the sins of our youth, nor our transgressions, but in thy great mercy look upon our desolation, the sharpness of our afflictions, and the reproach our sins have earned, and forgive us. Restore our souls; lead us in thy truth; teach us thy way; show us thy paths; make thy face to shine upon us, and be gracious unto us; and bring us out of all our distresses.

O Lord Jesus Christ, thou Son of David, who didst prophesy thy Passion and death, have mercy upon us. Open our sin-darkened eyes to behold thy glory and to rejoice in thy salvation. Bring divine light to our blinded souls, that we and all men may see in thee all the treasures of heavenly wisdom and knowledge. Teach us to pray. Give us faith that we may believe in thy power, in thy goodness and love; that thou art able to grant our petitions, and art willing to save unto the uttermost them that come unto the Father by thee.

O Holy Spirit, Lord and Giver of life, who by thy inspiration hast delivered us from the power of darkness and translated us into the kingdom of Christ, give us thy grace. Enlighten our understanding Grant unto us the spirit of a great faith, an abiding hope, and a pure love. Teach us of the great love wherewith Christ hath loved us, and guide us so that we may walk in that light.

O God, Father, Son, and Holy Spirit, in whom we live and move and have our being, bless this day to our growth in grace. Bless this house, that it may be continually a place where thine honor dwells, thy Name is praised, and thy truth is proclaimed. Bless our homes, that they may be rooted and grounded in love and every good work. Help all those among us who may be enduring any affliction, trial, or adversity, and reveal the exceeding greatness of thy power to all who believe.

Look in mercy, O Lord, thou who art the Lord of all the living and of all the dead, upon the nations of the earth, and cause all peoples and rulers to yield to thy authority that they may obtain lasting peace, true progress, and spiritual prosperity. Grant thy almighty aid to the hungry, the homeless, the stranger, the oppressed, the orphan, and the imprisoned everywhere. Cause thy church to this end to go forth to the nations preaching thy Gospel with courage and boldness under thy Holy Spirit, and manifesting by works of love and compassion thy grace and glory.

Now unto him whose name we bear, whose doctrine we confess, and whom, though we now see but darkly, we shall one day see face to face, even Jesus Christ, be honor and glory forever. Amen.

ash wednesday

Blessed be thou, O Lord, and blessed be thy Name forever and ever. Thine, O Lord, is the greatness, and the power, and the victory, and the majesty. Thine, O Lord, are heaven and earth, and thou art God over all. Holy art thou and righteous in all thy works. Thou lovest righteousness and hatest iniquity, and hast commanded a just recompense for all transgression. Thou hast declared the decree: The wages of sin is death; and if thou, O Lord, shouldst mark iniquities, who of us can stand? There is none that doeth good; and our righteousness is an unclean thing. But there is forgiveness with thee, that thou mayest be feared.

Wherefore, O heavenly Father, we acknowledge our transgression; and our sins are ever before us. The good that we would, we do not; and the evil which we would not, we have done. We have transgressed thy holy Word. In thought, word, and deed, that which was good we have corrupted; and in that which was wicked we have found pleasure. We have disdained the pure and loved the evil. The holiest joys and happiness that thou hast granted to us, O God, we have marred by our disobedience. We have sinned against heaven and in thy sight, and are unworthy to be thy children.

We come before thee, humbly trusting in thy promise that if we confess our sins, thou art faithful and just to forgive us our sins and to cleanse us from all unrighteousness. We plead the merits of thine only-begotten Son who called sinners to repentance. For the sake of his innocent sufferings and death, pardon us. Wash us in his precious blood from our iniquity, and free us from our sin. Turn us from our transgression. Save us from our folly. Deliver us from our wilfulness. By thy Spirit lead us from the arid, fruitless deserts of our lives to the grace of our Lord Jesus, as to a stream of living water. Refresh our souls in him, and restore unto us the comfort of his cross, wherein thou hast reconciled us unto thyself.

Shower thy blessing upon thy church. Endow it with every grace and let it flourish in every land in true faith and good works.

Look with favor upon our nation and crown it with virtue and godliness. Cleanse it of iniquity, and turn it to righteousness. Strengthen and uphold all in authority, and bind us together in justice and freedom.

Give us strong, pleasant homes, where, in all our common tasks, each one serves thee, and all is done to thy glory.

*Let now thy benediction fall upon us as we come to thy holy table. And as, by partaking of this bread and the fruit of the vine, we remember Christ our Lord, grant us a faithful recollection of all that he has done for us, and give us thankful hearts to praise, serve, and obey him.

For all who seek thy mercy and help, the sick and the aged, the lonely and the weary, the disheartened and the discouraged, we pray. Supply all their need according to thy riches in Christ Jesus, and grant them a joyful issue out of all their trials.

Vouchsafe unto all here assembled who have brought thee the sacrifices of broken spirits and contrite hearts, the fullness of thy mercy in the saving knowledge of our dear Redeemer, Jesus Christ, in whose Name we pray all these things. Amen.

---

*If the Lord's Supper is observed.

fiRSt sunday

O almighty God, heavenly Father, who didst appoint us who confess the Name of thy Son to preach his death until he comes again, we come unto thy throne of grace, humbly trusting in thy mercy.

We thank thee that thou hast given us a high priest, even Jesus Christ, who knows our infirmities, having borne them; who understands our temptations, having endured them; and who learned obedience by the things which he suffered.

O Lamb of God, who as sacrifice wast slain for the sins of the world, becoming the Author of eternal salvation to all who obey thee, teach us obedience. Give us such faith that we may obey to the uttermost all thy gracious and life-giving commands. Fill us with a true love to thee so that all fear of holy submission to thy Word is overcome. Grant us such trust that we, hearkening to thy voice, may find the true joy of conforming our wills to thy holy will.

O Holy Spirit, if we are led into the wilderness of temptation, deliver us by thy power and save us from all evil. Suffer us not in our times of testing to fall from thy grace. Help us to wrestle daily against the powers of darkness which manifest themselves in every circumstance or position in life. Overthrow the tempter, Satan, in every assault on our souls. Make us strong in thee and, by the example of the Lord Jesus, show us the victorious power of thy holy Word.

And as we of thy church, O God, are tenderly permitted to be workers together with thee in the saving of men, grant that we may receive thy grace for our own regeneration before we seek it for others. If there be any here in our midst who have not heeded thy call, grant, O Lord, thy power, that they may on this day heartily repent, believe the Gospel, and receive thy mercy.

Let thy blessing rest upon our homes. Give all parents wisdom to see the influence of character, and grace to be true followers of him who is the Light of the world, so that by their manner of life and conversation they may be worthy lights unto their children.

Bestow thy Spirit upon our country, O Lord, that in every office and calling, by every human virtue and divine grace, we may show forth thy praises, thy power, and thy glory.

And forasmuch as thou didst make the Captain of our salvation perfect through sufferings, if any among us be afflicted with suffering and pain, grant that they may learn of thy love and receive thy fatherly chastening. If any be sorrowful, give them the comfort of thy promises. If any be in need, show thyself the Source of all good. If any be dying, give them the confidence that though the earthly house of this tabernacle be dissolved, we have a building of God, eternal in the heavens.

Now, O Father, give thine angels charge over all thy people, to minister to their salvation, and to bring them safely through this world to that eternal kingdom which thou hast prepared for all them that love thee. In the Name of Jesus Christ, thy Son, our Lord. Amen.

second sunday

Almighty God, the Father of our Lord Jesus Christ, who dwellest not in temples made with hands, and who hast created all things, both visible and invisible, by thy mighty Word, grant us a true faith. Help us to know that without faith it is impossible to please thee, and that he who would come to thee must believe that thou art the living God, and that thou art the rewarder of them that diligently seek thee. Bring us to the understanding that thou hast the whole world in thy hand, and that none of us lives unto himself, and no man dies unto himself, for we are thine, and all is thine. Grant also that we may see that man's chief end is to believe in thee and in him whom thou didst send, even our Lord Jesus.

Thou hast spoken unto us by him; may we hear and obey him. Thou hast given us an example in him; may we walk in his steps. Thou hast bidden us to receive him in faith; may we open our hearts to his gracious indwelling. Thou hast told us that none comes unto thee but by him; may we see him as the Way to thy mercy seat. And thou hast called us to worship him; may we give him our love, our praise, and our adoration. We thank thee, O Father, that thou hast not appointed us to wrath, but to obtain salvation by our Lord Jesus Christ, who died for us. May we ever live together with him.

Now, O God, in the Name of him who gave himself for us that he might redeem us from all iniquity, help us to walk in obedience to thy commandments, to prove all things and hold fast to that which is good, to abstain from every appearance of evil. O God of all grace, by thy Son, our Savior, sanctify us wholly, that in spirit and soul and body we may be preserved blameless unto the coming of our Lord Jesus Christ.

And as thou wilt have all men to be saved and come to the knowledge of the truth, stir up thy church to send men and women to preach the Gospel at home and abroad. Endow thy people with the heart and vision to pray, give, and labor for the salvation of all men.

We make intercession for all men: for all in authority, that they may have respect unto thy holy will; for all who know not Jesus as Savior, that they may hear and believe the Gospel; for all who are in danger, that they may be preserved from harm. May all, in every land, dwell together in brotherhood and peace.

Grant that our homes may be tabernacles of thy Spirit. Make all who reside therein increase and abound in love one toward another. To all mothers give the grace of spiritual wisdom; to all fathers the gift of a good conscience; to all children the spirit of obedience.

Upon all, O Lord, who are here in thy house this day, have mercy. Forgive us our transgressions. Support the weak. Correct the disobedient. Against all evil and adversity that vex our souls or bodies, grant us thy aid.

These things we ask in the Name of thy Son Jesus who gave his life a ransom for us all that he might bring us unto thee. Amen.

thirò sunòay

Lord God most holy, who dwellest in the heavens, without whom there is no help, and with whom there is no danger, be thou the Guardian and Defender of all who lift up their souls unto thee, and who in their desolation or affliction seek thy mercy.

We thank thee for the love of Jesus and that in his compassion and grace he freely gave himself as the propitiation for our sins, yielding up his perfect life as an offering for our redemption and salvation. We thank thee for the finished work of our Lord: his holy life, his blessed example, his gracious teaching, his loving companionship, and his atoning death. With grateful hearts we thank thee for the willing spirit in which he gave himself as thy suffering Servant, fulfilling all the demands of thy holy law and righteous government, and satisfying the handwriting of ordinances against us.

Grant us thy Holy Spirit that we may have inheritance in thy eternal kingdom. Help us to imitate the example of Christ and to walk in love. Grant that as children of the heavenly light we may earnestly repent of our sins, forsake the ways of darkness and error, and follow in the paths of goodness, righteousness, and truth. With thy finger cast out all demons of uncleanness that assault us. Fill our souls with holiness, love of thy Word, and every pure grace and virtue.

Let thy hand, O Lord, rest upon thy church to prosper and defend it. Give success to all who sow the seed of thy Word, proclaim the glorious Gospel of salvation, and in Christ's Name minister to the souls and bodies of men. Give faithfulness to thy people that they may labor earnestly with Christ to gather his harvest into his eternal kingdom.

Stretch forth thy mighty arm to rule and direct our government, and give wisdom and integrity to all who bear the sword, that our nation may be kept in peace, and that righteousness and justice may everywhere prevail. Put down all oppressors, tyrants, and godless governments throughout the world, and turn the hearts of all enemies of thy truth to the acceptance of thy Word.

O Lord, great art thou and greatly to be praised.

For all who are in any want of body or soul, for all of our loved ones who are in distant places, for all who have strayed from thy truth, for all who are in temptation, for all who are suffering sickness and pain, for all who mourn, we pray. Pour down thy blessings upon them according to their need. Hear their prayers. Comfort them with thy presence. Unite us all in one spirit in thy church on earth and finally in thy courts in heaven. We pray, O Father, for these things in the Name of thy Son Jesus Christ. Amen

fourth sunday

Blessed art thou, O Lord, and blessed is thy Name forever and ever. Blessed art thou, O Lord, and blessed is thy Word forever and ever. Blessed art thou, O Lord, and blessed is thy Son Jesus forever and ever.

O God, we praise thee for all thy mercies. We thank thee that thou hast redeemed our life from destruction and crowned us with loving-kindness; and that thou hast not dealt with us after our sins, nor rewarded us according to our iniquities. Out of thine unspeakable grace and mercy, thou didst give thine only-begotten Son to be made sin for us, and to suffer for our transgressions, so that we might have everlasting life. We bless and praise thee that through Christ we are delivered from the bondage of the Law into the glorious liberty of thy sons, evermore having access boldly to thy throne of grace, there to obtain mercy and find grace to help in time of need.

Grant that we who are here gathered for thy worship, seeking thee while thou mayest be found, calling upon thee while thou art near, may repent of our evil, forsake all sinful thoughts and ways, and find that thou wilt abundantly pardon us for Jesus' sake.

And as thou, O Lord, art mindful of the necessities of all men, giving both the righteous and the ungodly their daily bread, make us sensible of thy providence and enable us to receive thy benefits with thanksgiving. Upon all that which in due season thou givest us, we ask thy favor and blessing that these thy gifts may support our bodies and show forth thy love and care. O Lord, keep us in health, to the end that we may serve thee in this life and in the world to come, through him who is the Bread from heaven, even Jesus Christ.

Cause thy gospel to be preached in all lands, and in every tongue. Maintain thy church in union with Jesus Christ in the true faith. Bless our schools, that all teachers may both acknowledge and serve thee, and that their pupils may find in thee the treasures of life and truth. Give wisdom and counsel to all who in the government of this land have authority over us, so that we may worship and serve thee without hindrance, and live in peace and righteousness.

Deliver us from the works of the wicked and preserve us in all dangers through which we must pass. To all who suffer sickness, pain, disease, affliction, or any adversity of body, mind, or spirit, give thou the strength that shall enable them to bear their cross and the spirit of him who taught us to say, "Thy will be done." In his glorious Name and for his kingdom's sake, we pray these things. Amen.

passion sunday

O Lord God, almighty and ever-living King of all creation, who art the God of Abraham, Isaac, and Jacob, and the Father of our Lord Jesus Christ, whom all the hosts in heaven praise and glorify, hear our prayer.

For the revelation of thy matchless love in the gift of thy Son, for the unsearchable wisdom which ordained his lifting up on the cross, for his high priestly sacrifice of his own body on the tree, for the gift of eternal redemption through his Passion, for the promise of eternal inheritance through his death, for the purging of our consciences from dead works by his obedience, and for his sanctifying grace, we thank thee, O God.

Grant that, under the new and better testament sealed by his agony and death, he may mediate to us thy richest blessings, the forgiveness of all our sins, deliverance from death and the power of the devil, and the assurance of everlasting life. Vouchsafe this mercy to each life here present before thee this day.

O God, we praise thee for the wondrous love, the beauty of the holiness, and the infinite power of Christ our Savior. We thank thee that thou hast spoken through him the words of life. We beseech thee to help us at all times to be faithful to his Word, and to be obedient to his commandments, that we may never taste the bitterness of death. Help us faithfully to honor him by faith and life, by word and deed. Grant that we may see in him eternal Godhead, Deity Incarnate, the everlasting "I Am" of heaven, uncreated, unchangeable, self-existent, the same yesterday, today, and forever. Inspire us to love and worship him in spirit and in truth.

Out of thine infinite goodness lift up thy church, O God, that it may be saved from all weakness and failure and empowered for holy service. Govern the nations of the earth, that man may live everywhere without fear of his neighbor. Give thy grace to our homes and schools, that youth may be trained for usefulness in this life and for entrance into the life hereafter. Bless all who labor with mind or hand in providing the necessities by which we must live, and give them the understanding that in all human toil we are accountable to thee. Help us to use our gifts as thy stewards. Forgive us all our transgressions. Be thou the Comforter of the suffering and afflicted, the Sun of the aged, the Supply of the needy, the Protector of the fatherless, and the Savior of all men. In the Name of Jesus Christ our Redeemer. Amen.

palm sunday

O God, heavenly Father, into thy presence we come with thanksgiving and joy. Thou art a great God. In thy hand are the deep places of the earth; the strength of the hills is thine also. The sea is thine and thou didst make it; and thy hands formed the dry land. Thou didst speak and it was done. Thou didst command and it stood fast. Thou sendest forth thy Word, and that whereunto it is sent is done.

In this holy hour we thank and praise thee that thou didst send to us thine incarnate and living Word, Jesus Christ, thy Son, who for the joy that was set before him endured the cross and despised the shame. Grant that as we look unto him we may, by his example, be neither weary in well-doing, nor faint in heart, nor murmuring when we are chastened and corrected, nor despairing of thy mercy; but that as we partake of his suffering we may also in faithfulness and obedience partake of his resurrection.

Save us, O God, not by the works of righteousness which we have done, but by shedding upon us abundantly the washing of regeneration and the renewing of the Holy Spirit. Sanctify and redeem us from all transgression and purify us unto thyself.

And as thou hast set our iniquities before thee, and our secret sins in the light of thy countenance, by the mercy of him who was offered to bear the sins of many, pardon us by his wounds and heal us with his stripes.

We are thy people and thou our God. Put then thy Law into our minds and write it into our hearts; put the song of salvation into our souls and clothe us with the garments of praise, that with joy we may declare: "Blessed is he that cometh in the Name of the Lord; Hosanna in the highest."

Let thy church gather from far and near into the Zion of faith all who would be saved. Send forth laborers, therefore, to preach thy Word in truth and to show forth the Name of Jesus as the only Name given under heaven whereby we must be saved. Prosper their witness in all the world, that all may know thee, from the least to the greatest.

Grant to this congregation, and to all who worship here, strength of purpose in thy holy service, that they may seek with willing minds and pure hearts the building and strengthening of thy kingdom.

We pray for all who are in sickness, pain, anxiety, fear of death, or sorrow. Be with them when they pass through the waters of trouble. Let them trust in thee, for thou wilt deliver them.

Now unto thee, O God, who art able to keep us from falling and to present us faultless before the presence of thy glory with exceeding joy, to the only wise God, our Savior, be glory and majesty, dominion and power, both now and forever. Amen.

monday

O God, who art our Life and Salvation, our Refuge and Fortress, the only source of all true strength and hope, from whom all good works and just counsels proceed: We thank thee that thou didst give us Jesus Christ, thine only-begotten Son, who, when he hid his glory, came down from heaven, took upon himself our flesh and humbled himself, so that, in suffering the afflictions of the body, the adversities of the soul, and the contradiction of sinners, he might thus purchase us with his blood and bring us to glory.

We thank thee that in him thou hast forgiven the iniquities of thy people and covered their sins. Grant that, following his example, we may ever live unto righteousness and patiently endure every adversity. Teach us to set our affection on things above, disdaining all love of the world, and to hold fast to the blessed promise of eternal life through Christ our Lord. Let thy Holy Spirit ever direct our thoughts, that we, obedient to his counsel, may be children of the light.

We beseech thee to bless all who trust in the merciful merits of Jesus Christ for salvation. We pray thy blessing upon all the schools of the church and upon all the charitable works of thy people, that in all things Christ may be honored.

Imbue us with zeal to perform thy will and to proclaim the glorious Gospel of our Savior to all the world. Grant that as Christ is lifted up, multitudes may be drawn to his faith and find healing in his cross.

For all in any want of body or soul we pray. Visit them with thy salvation, bestow upon them the strength and consolation of thy grace, and uphold them in every trial with thy free Spirit.

Grant us now, O God, forgiveness of our sins, a stronger faith, and a cleaner and purer life. Give us that peace which passes all understanding, for Jesus' sake. Amen.

tuesday

Almighty God, heavenly Father, who hast loved us beyond our understanding and cared for us beyond our deserving, and who hast commended thy love to us in that thou didst send thine only-begotten Son to be a ransom for sin, graciously hear our prayer.

We thank thee, dear Father, for the bitter sufferings and death of Christ Jesus, our Savior, which he bore without complaint, opening not his mouth to murmur, but enduring silently the pain and anguish, that he might witness a good profession before many witnesses. We confess that it was for us that he suffered and was led as a lamb to the slaughter. We acknowledge that he was bruised for our iniquities and wounded for our transgressions. We lament our sins and repent of our love of the world, lust of the flesh, lust of the eyes, and pride of life.

Turn our eyes to the cross from whence comes the light to lead us out of all our trials. Give us grace to overcome the dominion of the devil and power to fight the good fight of faith. Grant us thy Holy Spirit, that our hearts and lives may be sanctified unto thee. May we wholly trust for our salvation in the merits of Christ and, clinging to his cross, find thy loving purpose reaching into the depths of our souls and redeeming and cleansing us for the joys of heaven.

Abide with thy church in all the world, O Lord, that like the eternal hills she may be unshaken. Strengthen the walls of this holy house of prayer that thy people may find here in thy presence courage, inspiration, and solace.

Bless our native land and guard with watchful eye her honor and security, that her people may love and trust in thee.

Bring light through thy Word to our homes, so that we, thy children, with thankful devotion, may ever know thee more truly and serve thee more purely.

Hear and sanctify all the prayers which each of us offers to thee in his heart, that in all things thy kingdom may come, thy will be done, and thy holy Name be glorified. Bless and keep us ever thine. We ask, O God, these petitions humbly, penitently, believingly, in the Name of Christ our Lord, whom to see is to see thee, whom to hear is to hear thee, whom to love is to love thee. Amen.

wednesday

O God, who art our Light and Salvation, our Refuge and Fortress, and the Strength of our life; and who didst deliver up thy Servant Jesus to be reckoned among transgressors and to be betrayed by cruel and wicked hands, to suffer and be crucified, in order that whosoever believes on him may have the remission of sins, hear us as we pray.

We thank thee that thou hast forgiven the iniquity of thy people and covered their sin through the atonement made by Christ our Lord at Calvary. We thank thee for his patience and his suffering, his life and love, his ministry and mercy. We praise thee that he, the Way, the Truth, and the Life, was delivered for our offenses; that through his innocent sufferings and death he tasted death for every man that all men may be reconciled unto thee. We give thanks unto thee that he, who was despised and rejected of men, a Man of Sorrows and acquainted with grief, is the all-sufficient sacrifice for our sins, the great manifestation of thy love, and the Deliverer through whom thou hast accomplished our eternal salvation.

Help us now, O God, to serve thee by word and life more faithfully each day, to resist and overcome all temptation to do evil, and to receive from thee a new heart and a new spirit. Make us mindful of all that thy Son has done for us and to love him more. Forgive us our sins, and lead us safely through the problems that we face each day. Give us stronger faith, and strengthen us to bear cheerfully our crosses, and to meet victoriously all our trials.

Vouchsafe unto us thy presence and nearness that in all perils of body or soul we may have the assurance of thy instant and loving care. Defend and protect us from all harm and danger, and grant that in every adversity the power of Christ may rest upon us.

From the throne and glory of thy kingdom, O God, look upon this land and preserve it from every evil. Manifest thy ineffable might and majesty to all the peoples of the earth that they may bow before thee in worship, and by their obedience to thy commandments honor thy Word and will. Subdue the unrighteous, and turn the hearts of the unbelieving. Show mercy to the hungry, the homeless, and the oppressed everywhere.

Grant thy favor to all in this congregation. Enter our homes and let thy Spirit prevail in every heart.

Bless the sick, the forsaken, the suffering, the anxious, and the perplexed, and give us all that victory in Christ which overcomes the world.

Now unto him who loved us and washed us from our sins in his own blood and has made us kings and priests unto God and his Father, unto him be glory and dominion forever and ever. Amen.

thursday

Heavenly Father, almighty God, who in thine unspeakable mercy hast provided divine knowledge and understanding for a needy world through Jesus Christ, the Bread from heaven, we thank and praise thee for thy goodness and loving-kindness.

Forgive us the multitude of our transgressions, and grant that we may receive the works of Christ in faith so that we may have perfect remission of all our sins. Take not thy Holy Spirit from us, but restore unto us the joy of thy salvation. Satisfy our souls with the Bread of Life, and grant that, believing in him, we may never hunger again. Cast us not by reason of our sin and faithlessness from thy presence, but receive us through Christ into thine everlasting kingdom. Overcome all pride and self-will in us that resist obedience to the example of Jesus, and give unto us a ready mind and a pure heart to follow in the way he has prepared for us. Remove the blindness from our spiritual eyes, that we may behold our true selves in the mirror of thy Word; and give us unfeigned repentance as we see ourselves as thou seest us. Thou seest all things, O Lord, and nothing is hid from thee. Our secret sins thou beholdest in the light of thy countenance. Therefore we cast ourselves down before thee, trust in thy mercy, and beseech thy grace, that the blood of Jesus Christ may cleanse and wash us of all our offenses.

Grant thy favor to thy church, O Father, that, being nourished by the true Manna which came down from heaven, it may have vision and strength to do thy will.

Let thy benediction rest upon all who feel the bitter pains of illness, the shame of conscience, the ache of sorrow, the sadness of separation, and the sting of death. Give unto all such as crave thy gracious help the ministry of thy holy angels now in this time and, in the end, entrance into thine eternal glory.

Now as we proclaim the Lord's Passion and death in the Communion of his Table, uniting our hearts and spirits in his faith and fellowship, grant us the earnest of thy presence, the confidence of thy mercy, and the hope of heaven. Through Jesus Christ, whose body we discern in these elements, and whose gifts we receive by his grace, we pray these things. Amen.

good friday

O God the Father almighty, who in the mystery of thine eternal counsel didst ordain thy Son to be our Sacrifice for sin, and upon whom thou didst lay the iniquity of us all, that in the gift of his life and in the Sacrament of his death, the remission of the sins of all who believe on him would be accomplished, grant us thy peace.

In this holy hour of meditation, when in humility we contemplate how great a salvation thou didst in mercy prepare for us, we thank thee for the revelation of thyself in thy Son, and for the manifestation in him of thy will and grace. We thank thee for the eternal words of spirit and life which he gave us, and for his heavenly doctrine; for the fulfillment in him of the law and the prophets, and for our deliverance from condemnation; for his sacrificial love, and for his perfect obedience; for his mercies of healing, and for his holy example of patience in suffering; for his willingness to endure the cross, and for his submission to death.

Grant that we may see, in the darkness that attended his dying, in the shaking of the earth and rending of the rocks, when nature itself mourned its Lord, how great an evil was done by the hands of men, how great a life was ended, how great a death was inflicted. But in the sundering of the veil of the Temple, and in the opening of the graves of the saints, show us our entrance through the innocent blood of Jesus into the heavenly Holy of Holies.

For all that he has done, for all that he has borne, for all that he has given us, for all that he has promised us, we thank thee, O Father.

From the ends of the earth, thy church, which Christ loved and for which he gave himself, bows in adoration and praise. From the depths of every believing and understanding heart the prayer of gratitude rises as incense to thy presence. From the ransomed and redeemed of every kindred and tongue and people and nation, the song of thanksgiving and worship ascends to heaven: Worthy is the Lamb that was slain to receive power and riches and wisdom and strength and honor and glory and blessing.

Heavenly Father, by all that we remember on this day of our Savior's Passion, grant us such instruction as we may need to secure our salvation. In his suffering show us that we must enter thy kingdom through much tribulation. In his wounds give us enlightenment and encouragement for all adversity. In his crucifixion teach us that they that are Christ's have mortified their vanities and lusts. By his death help us to prepare for ours. And in his burial help us to see that he who brought life and immortality to light for all who believe has also sanctified their graves.

Now, as we have received thy mercy and seen thy glory in the face of Jesus Christ, grant unto us, O God, the multiplying of thy grace through him who died, but who rose again and evermore reigns as King of heaven and earth. In his glorious Name. Amen.

saturday

O God, the Father of our Lord Jesus Christ, who for the transgression of thy people didst suffer thy Son to be stricken and smitten, the righteous for the unrighteous, that he might bring us unto thee, grant unto us a ready access in prayer to thy throne, so that we, coming unto thee in all boldness, may have the assurance of thy mercy.

In this solemn hour of our worship, as we await the anniversary of the day of our Lord's resurrection, help us to recall his suffering and death. As we commit ourselves body and soul into thy hand, vouchsafe unto us the deep serenity of spirit that was his. Grant unto us the true and living trust that he displayed, that we may ever find ourselves in thy holy and mighty keeping. Give us his perfect submission to thy fatherly will, that we, too, may keep our souls in tranquility and peace now and in the hour of our death.

When our day is done, and the sunset of life is upon us, and the evening shadows of our passing gather about us, help us in our helplessness to commit the keeping of our souls to thine eternal care. Vouchsafe unto us a quiet end, and grant that our bodies may rest in the earth in peace.

We contemplate in reverence the burial of thy Son Jesus Christ. We thank thee that as he sanctified our human body by his birth so also he sanctified our grave by his burial. When, in the time of our death, our bodies shall return to the earth from whence they came, bless that place, O God, and grant that we may at the last day rise therefrom to eternal life. Look upon the resting places of all our loved ones, and let them speak to us of the hope and joy of heaven in unison with all our beloved who departed in the true faith.

And as in these days of our Lord's burial, quickened in the spirit, he preached unto the imprisoned souls of all the dead who awaited his atonement, grant that the preaching of his church may continue in all the world, and bring to conversion multitudes who are imprisoned by sin and the power of the devil, that they may have the promise of life that now is and of that which is to come.

Give grace, heavenly Father, to all who are passing through the valleys of sin, sorrow, suffering, or other shadows of death, that they may trust in thy mercy and thus be delivered from their afflictions.

O God, we humbly beseech thee to forgive our manifold sins and iniquities. By the precious blood of Christ heal us, cleanse us, save us. Have mercy upon us, O Lord. Restore unto us the joy of thy salvation.

These and all other things which thou knowest we have need of, we pray in Jesus' holy Name. Amen.

AN EARLY SERVICE

EASTER DAY

Blessed art thou, O God and Father of our Lord Jesus Christ, who according to thine abundant mercy hast begotten us again unto a new and living hope by the resurrection of Jesus from the dead.

Thou hast transformed the night of doubt and sorrow into the new and eternal day of joy and gladness by the rolling of the stone from the door of the tomb. Thou hast brought life and immortality to light by the glad tidings that Christ is risen, that death has no power over him. Thou hast sent unto all dwelling in this world of darkness and the shadow of death the joyful hope of an inheritance incorruptible and full of glory. O God, we thank thee.

Thou hast delivered, from the grip of death, thy Son, who died for our sins, and hast raised him by thy power. Thou hast brought him forth as the First-fruits of all who sleep and given him the keys of death and hell. That which thou didst sow in dishonor and weakness, thou didst raise in glory and power. O God, we praise thee that through him thou hast taken away for us the sting from death, and victory from the grave.

Fill our hearts with the joy of the resurrection. Grant unto thy church and people everywhere the power of an endless life, that they may show forth thy praises. Bestow thy grace upon our homes, and bless them with Easter's consolation and hope. Send forth the conquering banner of Christ's victory into all the world, that nations may join the hosts of heaven in songs of triumph.

Guard us, O Lord, by thy power, that we may be kept in this holy faith. Wipe away all tears from our eyes. In every adversity and trial preserve us so that we fail not in receiving the blessings of Christ's ransom and the fruits of his resurrection. In the promise of Easter take from us all fear of death. Let the radiant beams of the Easter dawn's early light shine into the depths of our souls. Renew us by the Spirit of him who is the Way, the Truth, and the Life. Hold fast before our eyes the promise that in Christ our lowly bodies shall be fashioned like unto his glorious body, and that as we have borne the image of the earthly so shall we bear the image of the heavenly. And then when thou callest us to thy heavenly rest, may we sleep peacefully in Jesus, awaiting the sound of the trumpet, when the dead shall be raised incorruptible.

In the Name of our risen and ever-living Lord. Amen.

EASTER DAY

O thou God of peace, who hast brought again from the dead our Lord Jesus, the great Shepherd of the sheep, through the blood of the everlasting covenant, we thank and praise thee for thy mercy in his glorious resurrection.

Give us the radiant joy of the first Easter. Fill our hearts with its sublime announcement and precious promise. Make us glad in the heavenly tidings that he who died for our sins rose again for our justification; that because he lives, we too shall live; that death has no power over us; that he has abolished death and brought life and immortality to light.

Grant us a lively faith, that we may receive both the infallible proofs of his death and the infallible testimonies of his resurrection. And as thou hast declared that if we shall confess with our mouth the Lord Jesus and believe in our heart that thou didst raise him from the dead, we shall be saved, endow us with all such spiritual gifts as shall obtain for us thy salvation.

Order our steps by thy Word and quicken us by its power, that we, obeying thy commandments and trusting in thy promises, may receive the fullness of thy blessing both in this life and that which is to come.

Bestow thy gracious favor upon our homes and imbue our families with such a sense of thy goodness and manifold gifts, especially the gift of eternal life in thy Son, that Easter may be observed with the solemnity of sincere thanksgiving and celebrated with the joy of blessed hope.

Have dominion over all the nations of the earth, O Lord, and bring them to thine obedience, that all men, from the least to the greatest, walking in thy love and fear, may find him who has the words of eternal life.

For thy church we pray: Grant that everywhere it may have faithful and true shepherds who are not ashamed of that Gospel which is power unto salvation; and endow all its members with the assurance of the resurrection faith, that as thou didst raise our Lord, so also by thy power thou wilt raise us. Grant that all believers throughout the world this day may find the fullness of thy grace and peace. Help all to be faithful unto death, that they may receive the crown of life. By thy Spirit make us, heavenly Father, perfect in every good work to do thy will, and work in us that which is well pleasing in thy sight, through Jesus Christ, to whom be glory forever and ever. Amen.

monday

O Lord God, our Strength, our Song, and our Salvation, glorious in holiness, fearful in power, wonderful in love, we thank thee for the marvelous fulfillment of the promise made unto the fathers in the resurrection of thy Son Jesus Christ from the dead.

Grant unto us the opening of our spiritual eyes that we may behold the glory of our Lord and receive from him the gift of life. Open to us thy Holy Scriptures, wherein we read that all that thou hast said by the prophets concerning the Christ, his suffering, death, and rising from the dead, has most truly come to pass. Open our hearts that the Sun of righteousness may impart light and healing to our sin-darkened lives.

Anoint thy church, O God, with the Holy Spirit and with power, and ever manifest thy presence to all who are gathered into its fold, that in worship and work it may proclaim thy Word and testify that thou hast ordained him now in this time to be the Savior of the world and in the end to be the Judge of the quick and the dead.

Let the festival of this Easter be celebrated in our homes, to the end that we may rejoice in our salvation and glory in the Christ who broke the bonds of death and opened for us the gates of everlasting life.

Send forth thy truth unto the far reaches of the earth and to every habitation of men, that they may know Christ's power over sin and hell and his victory over the grave.

If any amongst us have trouble, care, or sorrow, endow them with the joy and peace of a pure faith, the quietness and confidence of a true love, and the blessed hope of a heavenly rest that awaits the people of God.

Make us mindful of those most dear to us who in faith have entered thy rest; may our comfort and consolation be that as they have truly served thee, O Father, here in this world so they shall rejoice and praise thy redeeming love forever. Grant that we may meet them in the joy of heaven, through Jesus Christ, who will come again and receive us also unto himself. Amen.

EASTER

ſIRST SUNDAY

O God of all grace, mercy, and peace, who, by the resurrection of Jesus from the dead, didst declare him to be thy Son and our Savior, and who, by the faithful testimony of the apostles, hast given us assurance that our faith stands upon a most true and sure record, grant us the witness of thy Spirit, that our hearts may rest in thy truth.

We thank thee for the unspeakable gift of eternal life in thy Son. Preserve and defend us from all assaults upon our souls, so that we may hold fast to the profession of our faith. Deliver us from doubt and despair. Save us from vain philosophies and worldly wisdom. Give us thy doctrine, the Spirit of truth, and the mind of Christ.

We lift up our hearts to thee in thanksgiving for thy Word. Grant us so to desire its pure and refreshing nourishment that we may daily bring forth the fruits of righteousness in our pilgrimage upon earth. Illumine us by its heavenly light and instruct us by its saving truth. Help us therein to find Jesus; and though we behold him not, save with the eyes of faith, lead us to love him and to rejoice in him with joy inexpressible and full of glory, and grant that we may receive the end of our faith, even the salvation of our souls.

Breathe upon thy church, that it may faithfully preach thy Word and proclaim the Gospel of our risen Savior with courage and diligence in all lands and to all people.

Have respect, O Lord, unto our prayer for all the schools of the church, its colleges and seminaries, and its parish schools, that they may bring forth youth who walk in the way of thy commandments and are obedient to thy holy will.

Hearken unto the supplications that may rise secretly in our hearts for some special help or favor, and give us the assurance of thy mercy. And if, in thine unsearchable wisdom, thou hast permitted a cross to be laid on any of us, assure us that thou wilt not permit us to be tried above that we are able, but wilt strengthen us therein through the grace of Jesus Christ.

Forgive now the sins of thy people. Strengthen the doubting and the faithless. Bring back the forgetful and the wayward. And comfort the anxious and the distressed.

And as we go from this hallowed place this day, grant unto us all thy peace.

All this we pray in the Name of Christ our Lord. Amen.

second sunday

O Lord our God, how great is the goodness which thou hast laid up for them that fear thee; how good are the things which thou hast prepared for them that love thee. Give us thy holy fear and love, that we, through Jesus Christ thy Son, may obtain those glories which our eyes have not seen, nor our ears heard, neither have entered our hearts.

We thank thee for the grace which sent Christ the Good Shepherd into the world to lay down his life for the sheep, to ransom us by his blood from the power of evil, to redeem us by his Passion from the deserved consequences of our sins, and by his cross to liberate us from the fear and bondage of death.

We praise and bless thee for his resurrection and the bright and glorious promise that all who hear his voice and follow him shall, in the likeness of his resurrection, also be raised.

Accept our thanksgiving for his compassion on us, who were like sheep without a shepherd, going astray, but who are now, through thy great mercy, returned unto the Shepherd and Bishop of our souls.

For thy forgiveness and the remission of all our sins, for the promise of thy peace and the pledge of thy salvation, for thy presence and power, for thy loving-kindnesses and tender mercies, for every gift and grace in Christ Jesus, we thank thee, merciful Father.

Bestow upon thy church all such things as are needful to it, that it may be obedient to the example of its Savior and seek the lost sheep of the Israel of faith, raise the fallen, rescue the weary, comfort the faint, restore the erring, feed the hungry, clothe the naked, visit the imprisoned, shelter the homeless, and thus show forth the praises of him who has called us out of darkness into his marvelous light. Draw all thy people to a oneness of faith, doctrine, and spirit, that in obedience to truth, in loyalty to Jesus Christ, and in the concern for the prosperity of his kingdom, there shall be but one fold and one Shepherd.

In all parliaments and councils of nations, in all deliberations of commerce and industry, in all instruction in colleges and universities, in all civic and social life, give us, O God, the voice and leadership of the Good Shepherd. Suppress the vain boasts, the deceitful words, and the hollow glorying of men. Let the earth be still that it may hear and obey the Word of the Lord of life.

Direct our path through the sin, strife, and uncertainty of these times, O Lord. Grant us true faith and a godly heart. Strengthen the sick, support the weak, supply the needy, and show thyself a very present help in every necessity.

And when our last hour shall come, because our eyes have seen thy salvation, let us depart in peace according to thy Word, and receive us into everlasting glory, through Jesus Christ, thy Son and our Redeemer. Amen.

thiro sunoay

O Lord God, heavenly Father, who art mighty in power and infinite in majesty, who hast created the heaven and the heaven of heavens, and bringest out by name each star in the celestial host, as we enter into the courts of thy presence with thanksgiving and prayer, incline thine ear unto us, and in thy mercy hear us.

We give thanks unto thee, everlasting God, that thou didst glorify thy Son Jesus in his resurrection from the dead, after he had offered himself as Priest and as Sacrifice for all the world, laid himself upon the altar of the cross, and died to reconcile sinners unto thee. Grant us the blessings of his infinite grace and inexhaustible love.

We praise thee that thou didst transform the "little while" of the crucifixion sadness and defeat into the joy and victory of the resurrection. Help us to lay hold of Christ's promise of eternal life, and receive it in joy. Give us this glorious consolation by a true and living faith. Grant us the hope and assurance that our eyes shall yet behold him, when, according to thy promise, our Redeemer shall at the latter day stand upon the earth, and receive us and all who believe in him into the kingdom prepared from the foundation of the world.

And as the empty tomb has been the cradle of the church of Christ, we pray that all believers may be endowed with zeal to perform thy will so that thou mayest be glorified and multitudes turned from their sin to faith in our risen Lord.

Bestow thy favor upon our land. Give us a government that pre-

82

serves liberty, upholds justice, seeks righteousness, curbs lawlessness, and by thine ordinance bears its sword in courage and integrity. Let all Christian citizens in accordance with thy will accept their lawful obligations cheerfully and dutifully, giving respect to those in authority and honor to all men.

And as our eternal dwelling place is with thee, O Father, grant us, who are but strangers and pilgrims on earth, such a measure of thy power and grace that we may resist all evil, fight the good fight of faith, and in the end receive the victor's crown of life.

Give the comfort of thy promises to the sick, the sorrowful, the broken-hearted, and the perplexed. Cast out from our hearts all fear of death and the unknown. Instill in us patience in every adversity. And enable us to receive all thy many blessings in love and gratitude.

These things we ask in the glorious hope of an eternal day with thee, for the sake of Jesus Christ our Lord. Amen.

fourth sunday

Almighty God, the Father of our Lord Jesus Christ, who didst send thy Son into the world, not to be ministered unto, but to minister and to give his life a ransom for many, and who didst raise him by thy glory when he had offered the one sacrifice for sins forever, grant us a sure faith in him, that we may possess the blessed hope of eternal life.

For the multitude of thy mercies we thank thee, and pray that we may ever be mindful that every good and perfect gift is from above and comes from thee. Teach us that thy mercy is from everlasting to everlasting upon them that fear thee, and that there is no variableness nor shadow of turning in all thy kindness and compassion, for thou art the same yesterday, today, and forever.

We thank thee, O Father of Lights, for all spiritual and intellectual illumination and for the revelation of thy divine truth in Jesus Christ. Grant that all who are of the truth may come to him. Pour out upon us thy Spirit, that he may, through the engrafted Word, guide us into all truth by making known the mysteries of thy will, thine unchangeable purpose for the raising of fallen man, and the pure and perfect doctrines that pertain to our eternal salvation.

We thank thee for the gift of thy church and the fellowship of the saints. In order that it may be one, holy, Christian, and apostolic, keep it in the unity of the Spirit and the bond of peace, give it steadfast obedience to thy commandments, preserve it in union with Jesus

Christ in the true faith, and continue it in conformity with the inspired teaching of the apostles. Shower thy blessing upon it everywhere. Protect it from all its enemies. Prosper it in all its labors.

For the gift of the home we give thanks to thee. Let thy Spirit dwell in each house, that love and tranquility, joy and consolation, strength and virtue, may reign in undiminished glory.

For the gift of our noble and pleasant land, accept our thanks, O God. Stretch forth thy holy arm to defend it inwardly and outwardly from all who would bring it shame and reproach by reason of sin, from all who would overthrow it by strife and rebellion, and from all who would assault and destroy it by war.

For the gifts of our daily bread and all things needful for the wants and support of this present life, we thank thee. For the blessings of health and healing, for education and social joys, for friends and companions, for the beauties and powers of the earth and the wondrous marvels of the heavens, we thank thee.

Great art thou, O Lord, and great is thy goodness. Mighty art thou in all thy works, and glorious in thy salvation. Help us now and always to receive thy gifts with gratitude. Hear our prayers. Grant us thy graces, and finally receive us into everlasting communion with thee and with thine only-begotten Son Jesus Christ. In his Name we pray. Amen.

fifth sunday

O Lord God, whose divine thoughts and sublime ways are as far removed from ours as the heavens from the earth, who livest to bless and to communicate life, love, beauty, and joy throughout thy universe, and to receive with pardon thy penitent children, we praise and glorify thee for thy great goodness.

We give thee our heartfelt thanks for the precious gift of thy Son Jesus, whom thou didst send that we might have life and have it more abundantly, and who, to accomplish his mission, innocently suffered in meekness and humility the afflictions of this life, took our sins and infirmities in his own body, and bore them unto death upon the cross. For this great salvation, for our deliverance from the dominion of death by his resurrection, and for the sweet hope of heaven, we glorify thee, O Lord God, and sing forth the honor of thy Name.

And now, trusting in the promise of thy Son that whatsoever we shall ask of thee in his Name thou wilt grant, we beseech thee to move our hearts to such love and affection for our Savior that in all things we will gladly hear his Word and willingly obey his doctrine.

Send forth thy Word, O God, into all the world, that in the power of its sacred truth it may accomplish that whereunto thou hast sent it, bringing salvation where it is obeyed, condemnation where it is rejected, and judgment on the deeds of all men in this present time for eternity.

Bless thy church and let it be, both here in this congregation and everywhere, a loving union of the faithful, a holy communion in sacred things, a people of faith and prayer, exercising a true religion in the performance of every merciful work.

As thou dost govern the nations on this earth, look in mercy upon them and turn them into the ways of justice, righteousness, and peace.

Especially do we beseech thy gracious favor upon our land. Bestow upon our president, our councilors and legislators, and all our magistrates such endowments of mind and heart that they may perform their several duties with diligence, equity, honor, and intelligence. Defend us from all enemies within and without. Remove all grievances from our midst. Inspire obedience to law. Overthrow all workers of unrighteousness, and grant us a love of holiness and purity. For all who toil in industry we pray that they may prosper and receive the fruit of their labor. To all who serve thee in the professions grant the satisfaction of a noble work. Bless the farmers and all who produce the fruits of the soil, that they may have favorable weather and a bountiful harvest, and ever acknowledge thee who art the Giver of our daily bread.

Bless all our loved ones. Especially do we remember before thee the sick and those who mourn. Let them seek thee and receive thy gracious help and be mercifully delivered from all their distresses.

Now, O Lord, keep us steadfast, unmovable, always abounding in thy work, forasmuch as we know that in thee our labor is not in vain. In the Name of Jesus we pray always. Amen.

the ascension

O Lord God, our Father, who art our Strength and Song, and who hast prepared for us a well of salvation in Jesus Christ thy Son, who through the eternal Spirit did make himself an offering for the sins of the world, we thank thee for thy great mercy.

Most heartily we praise thee for the life of grace and truth that he lived among us. We thank thee for his perfect revelation of thee, and for the unfolding of thy glorious purposes and solemn designs. Grant us to believe all that he has taught us and to do all that he has commanded us.

Accept our thanks also for his mighty works and merciful deeds. Help us by these signs to see surely and certainly that in thee we live and move and have our being, and that all things are done in thy power.

Most especially we thank thee for his death and resurrection. By thy Spirit enable us to receive his sacrifice for our redemption and to trust in him for the gift of eternal life.

Grant now, as we celebrate with joy the ascension of our Lord, that even as thou didst raise him to the right hand of thy power and majesty in heavenly places, so may we ever exalt and praise him in adoration and prayer, and find in him the springs of gladness and devotion.

Lift the eyes of thy church heavenward to see, beyond mortal sight, him who ever lives to make intercession for the saints, and grant thy people hope and confidence in the exceeding greatness of his power toward us who believe. Quicken us who are baptized with the Holy Spirit, to witness to the saving grace of Jesus to multitudes at home and abroad and to preach the Gospel to every creature.

Establish Christ's kingdom in every nation, and from the four corners of the earth turn the hearts of men to his faith and obedience, so that every knee may bow and every tongue confess that he is Lord.

Maintain our land in righteousness and peace. Let our rulers ever be men that love and honor thee. Give unto all our schools the spirit of wisdom and revelation in the knowledge of him. Bless all institutions of mercy, and uphold and further all good works. Deliver us from war and pestilence, and spare us from greed, rebellion, and lawlessness. Give our people a sincere love of piety and peace, and thus guide and prosper us.

We pray for thy mercy upon all who are in any way afflicted. Especially do we beseech thy gracious help for the sick. Give them the confidence that whatsoever they ask in accordance with thy will thou wilt grant. May they pray with all patience and trustfulness.

And now, O God, as this same Jesus that was taken into heaven shall come again in like manner as he ascended, let our hearts rise thither in gratitude and love, and help us to look for his appearing again to receive us to himself, and to prepare in watchfulness and prayer for his return.

In the Name of Jesus Christ, which Name is above every name, we offer these petitions. Amen.

THE SUNDAY AFTER

the ascension

Almighty God, our Light and our Salvation, we adore and praise thee for thy manifold works of love and mercy toward all the children of men, but especially for the gift of thine only-begotten Son, to whom thou gavest triumphant ascension into heaven to sit upon thy right hand, far above all principalities and powers, and a name that is above every name, not only in this world, but in that which is to come.

We thank thee that thou hast thus crowned him with glory for his perfect life, his loving obedience, his innocent sufferings, and his redeeming death. And as thou hast raised him as King over all the earth and Head over all the church, may we also confess that he is the true Lord of our hearts and the only Savior of men.

For this pure and holy intention, O God, may thy Holy Spirit give us understanding and knowledge concerning the things that pertain to thine eternal kingdom. Comfort and strengthen us by the light of heavenly truth, as the Spirit illumines our minds. Through thy Spirit teach us of thy manifold grace in Jesus, and lead us into the paths of brotherly love, fervent charity, and willing generosity. Let him inspire us to give heed to this hour of history and to this time in our lives, and to watch and pray that we fall not into temptation. And in any testing of our faith, grant us by thy Spirit to be steadfast, unmovable, always abounding in the work of our Lord.

All who serve in thy church endow in full measure with the mind of the Spirit, that Christ may be confessed with all faithfulness, his cross uplifted, and his Gospel declared as the only power unto salvation. Grant thy ministers and missionaries grace and power, and thy people zeal for thy house.

Give thy blessing to all parents, that they may be wholesome examples to encourage their children in love toward thee, in the practice of virtue, in the desire to pursue learning to its foundation, and in usefulness to thy church and to all men.

Pour out thy Spirit upon our nation, that our people may dwell in peaceful homes and serve thee in all godliness and honor. To this end bestow thy benediction on all who labor with mind or hand, that they may work with diligence and honesty and receive the just reward of their toil. Give a sanctified intelligence to all in government, that they may perform their duties in such manner as to receive thy favor.

Hear the prayers of all who are afflicted with any adversity. In the quiet hours of the night when there is no one to lighten the weight of pain, loneliness, and anxiety, grant unto them strength and hope in the assurance of thy love, thy power, and thy nearness.

And now, as we go from this season of prayer, we give glory unto Jesus Christ, to whom be praise and dominion for ever and ever. Amen.

THE DAY OF PENTECOST

whitsunday

Almighty, eternal, heavenly Father, who hast poured out thy Holy Spirit upon thy church, that he may abide with it forever, preserving it in the true faith of thy Holy Word, and enlightening it with the knowledge of Jesus Christ, grant unto us, as we now call upon thy Name, all such things as may be necessary for our salvation.

We thank thee, O God, that by thy Spirit we have been called to faith in Jesus Christ, given power to believe thy Word, and gathered into the fellowship of thy holy church. Sanctify us that we, purged of our sins and unrighteousness, may be meet for the Master's use and prepared unto every good work.

To this end aid us, by the witness of thy Spirit, to know more deeply and truly the Holy Scriptures that we may become increasingly wise unto salvation; and help us to continue in their teachings. Enable us to flee from the prince of this world, and to follow, with all who serve thee in purity of heart, the things that make for righteousness, faith, charity, and peace. Kindle in us a fervent desire for all that is good, all that is holy, all that is true. Shed thy Spirit upon us, that we may love Jesus Christ our Savior with all our hearts and minds, keep his words with a good conscience, and find in each day the blessed experience of his nearness and abiding presence.

Let the sanctifying wisdom and power of the eternal Comforter descend upon thy church, that she may be strong in faith. Impart to her his seven-fold gifts of grace, that her elders may have bright hopes of the time when the earth shall be full of the knowledge of the Lord as the waters that cover the sea, and when her young men and maidens may be granted inward visions of the holy triumphs of the Gospel.

Stir up thy church, O Lord, and imbue it with zeal to seek the lost, to bind up the broken-hearted, to bring comfort to the imprisoned, to heal the afflicted, and to cheer all that mourn.

Give thy Spirit room in all homes, that he may lead every child who bears thy Name into the paths of love and obedience, and endow every parent with an understanding heart and gentle ways, so that together the family may adorn the doctrine of our Savior with godliness and honor.

Govern the nations upon the earth, and help them to acknowledge thy power, dominion, and righteous judgment, so that they may turn from their evil ways and live.

Give unto our land and all in authority firmness in the right and steadfastness in integrity, and be thou our Shield and Buckler.

To all in trial or tribulation, the sick, the weary, the oppressed, the fearful, the needy, and the lonely, give the peace of Christ. Let their cry come unto thee, and grant them all things needful. These things we pray in Jesus' Name. Amen.

monday

Almighty and everlasting God, who hast given thy Holy Spirit to testify to the truth that is in Christ Jesus, endow thy church with divine power and sanctify thy people now as they come to thee in prayer.

We praise thee for the most sublime and marvelous gift of light through the Holy Ghost. We thank thee for his inspiration of the prophets and the apostles. Grant that we may give heed to their witness, and that as Christ's words were thy words, so their words may also be to us thy words, and that we may continue steadfastly in their doctrine, in all wisdom and spiritual understanding.

We thank thee for the Spirit's preservation of the Holy Scriptures, which, remaining forever unbroken, are a lamp unto our feet and a light unto our path. May they so flourish in the world that new multitudes in this generation and those to come may embrace their truth and trust in the Savior who promises everlasting life to all who come unto thee by him.

We thank thee for the burning zeal thy Spirit has given unto chosen servants to spread thy Gospel throughout the nations. Grant us a like passion, so that men everywhere may sing thy praises and rejoice in thy salvation.

We pray thee, O God, that thou wouldst ever direct and rule our lives, so that we may increase daily in the knowledge and love of thee and of thy Son Jesus Christ. By thy Spirit's influence bring us to true faith, sincere repentance and sorrow for our sins, and to abiding peace and comfort in the knowledge of Christ's saving grace. Kindle within us a hearty desire for all that is right, pure, just, and holy. Sanctify us in body and soul, that, as temples of thy Spirit, we may be loyal to our Savior, faithful to his church, and steadfast in the works of love and mercy.

O heavenly Father, thou Light and Life immortal, let the radiant beams of thy glory lighten the darkness of this world. Make the hearts of all men in all lands thy dwelling place.

Grant preeminence to thy Word and truth throughout our country. Teach us thy way, and let us walk in thy fear. Help us to live in holiness, and save us from all unrighteousness. Bestow upon us the spirit of reverence, of mercy, of kindness, of peace, and of good will.

May the blessed Comforter and Counselor be with those among us who are passing through dark valleys and deep waters, that they may find in thee the strength of their life and their portion forever. Be thou, O God, the Guardian of all in danger, the Companion of all in loneliness, the Power of all in temptation, the Solace of all in sorrow, the Hope of all who despair, the Health of all who are sick, and the Friend of the friendless. Fill us with thy Holy Spirit for Jesus' sake. In his Name we pray. Amen.

TRINITY SUNDAY

O God, thou Fountain of all our blessings, who art from everlasting to everlasting, and who dwellest in majesty, honor, and glory, as the most blessed Trinity of Father, Son, and Holy Spirit:

We thank thee for the rays of divine light by which we have come to know thee, and for the wondrous mercy by which we have come to love thee. We thank thee that thou art the one, true, triune Godhead, eternal, immortal, invisible, in whom we live and move and have our being.

We bless thee, almighty Father. Thy glory filleth the heavens and thou coverest thyself with light as with a garment; thou madest all things and didst lay the foundations of the earth; and thy judgments and decrees in the whole universe declare and show forth thy power and glory. O Lord, how manifold are thy works; in wisdom thou hast made them all.

We worship thee, O Christ, thou only-begotten Son of the Father. Thou wast lifted up to draw all men unto thee, that whosoever believes in thee should not perish but have everlasting life; thou hast been exalted to the right hand of the Father and been given a Name which is above every name; thou hast been given a kingdom which cannot be moved, and now ever livest to make intercession for thy people. O Lord, how great is thy mercy; in love thou hast ransomed and redeemed us.

We praise thee, O Holy Spirit, thou Spirit of truth, who hast called us by the Gospel and hast led us into all truth; thou hast gathered us into thy church and sanctified us by thy grace. Thou hast strengthened us in the inner man and renewed us in the spirit of our minds. O Lord and Giver of life, how marvelous are thy gifts; in grace thou givest them all.

We pray, almighty God, that we may be enriched from the treasures of thy wisdom and knowledge. Open to us the Holy Scriptures, that we may grow in the understanding of thy will, render thee a more acceptable service, and attain a more perfect love and obedience. Grant us the new birth into thine eternal kingdom, and save us by the washing of regeneration and renewing of the Holy Spirit. And because thy judgments are unsearchable to our sinful minds and thy ways are past finding out, we do not ask to see the distant scene of the unveiled future, but only to have more faith in thee, O God. Grant us, therefore, a pure and inward vision of Jesus our Savior, so that we may know thy glory, that thou art a God of love and mercy, and of grace and truth, and trust wholly and only in thee for all things in all times and in every place.

Abide with thy church, O Lord, and make her people and pastors diligent in the vocation whereunto thou hast called her. Cleanse her of error, weakness, and disobedience, and purify her in faith and all good works.

Strengthen thy truth in our faltering hands, and give us a lively hope in thy bountiful promises. Grant us, through the merits of Jesus Christ, the remission of all our sins, and preserve us unto the coming of thy heavenly kingdom, when we shall see thee face to face and faith shall be perfected in heavenly knowledge. In the Name of Jesus Christ. Amen.

fIRST SUNDAY

O Lord God, King eternal, of whom, through whom, and in whom are all things, both in heaven and earth, and who in the trinity of thy Godhead art one God, one Lord, one Sovereign, and who upholdest all things by the Word of thy power:

We give thee our most heartfelt thanks for the multitude of thy mercies which thou hast so graciously showered upon us. Grant that we may ever be mindful of the magnificence of thy gifts and the vast ocean of thy love and kindness.

For this world, its beauty and its life; for the seasons and for the harvest; for the resources of the earth and the abundance of the sea; for love and friendship, home and family, land and government, and all the wholesome gifts of society; for the wondrous endowments of body and mind; for strength and growth; for skills and senses; for reason and intelligence, for vision and imagination, for memory and reflection, for health and healing; for all these, O God, we give thee our thanks and praise.

Most of all, we thank thee for thy great love and for the priceless gifts which thou hast given in Jesus Christ, thine only-begotten Son, whom thou didst send for our salvation. For the forgiveness of our sins through him, for our deliverance by his power from the dominion of death and the devil, and for the promise of life everlasting, we thank thee.

Grant, O Lord, that our spirits may be lifted up to thee in thanksgiving, and that we may love thee with all our heart and with all our soul, and with all our might. As thou didst first love us, so let us love thee, thy Word, and thy law. Teach us to set thee always before us and to walk as obedient children in thy holy commandments. And as we wrestle against the powers of spiritual darkness in all our temptations, give us the strength and the moral courage we need to win the victory of faith. Help us to meet every test of our love and faithfulness, and save us by thy mercy.

And as thou didst anoint thy church with the Holy Ghost and with power, help her everywhere throughout the world, amongst all peoples and tongues, to declare thy wonderful works, to the end that multitudes may come to thy light.

Look in mercy upon the nations of the world and grant them thy peace. Especially do we beseech thee that thou wouldst bless our own land. Give the spirit of wisdom and understanding to all who rule over us. Banish all vain ambition and love of power and luxury. In scenes of want and wrong, and in the haunts of strife and fear, let thy Spirit prevail, that men may live in brotherly love, bearing one another's burdens, and so fulfill the law of Christ.

Upon all our homes let the sunshine of thy love descend, and grant that our children may be reared in thankful devotion to thee, and all their days walk in thy praise.

We entreat thee, O loving Father, for thy mercy and grace upon all who face adversity or trial. Be thou the Health of the sick, the Joy of the sorrowing, the Staff of the aged, the Companion of the lonely, and the Strength of the weak. Grant us all these petitions, O Lord, and whatsoever we may ask in the depths of our own hearts, for the sake of him who died that we might ever live unto thee. Amen.

second sunday

Almighty God, our heavenly Father, who art our Strength and Stay, upholding all creation by thy power, sustaining the earth and all who dwell therein by thy love, and enlightening the hearts of thy children by thy truth, grant us thy fear and love, that we, walking in thy heavenly precepts, may attain the beginning of all true wisdom.

Father, we thank thee for the manifestation of thy majesty in all the universe, in which we see thine infinite power, and in which we discern thy wisdom. Give us, we pray, ears to hear the music of thy creation and eyes to see the wonders of thy glory.

We praise thee for the revelation of thyself in thy law, in which thou dost teach us thy holy will and by which thou dost govern the world. Grant that it may ever instruct us in righteousness, that we may give heed to its commandments, and that we may not fall under its judgments.

We bless thee for the visions of the prophets, for by them thou hast unveiled thy grace and given us great and precious promises. We beseech thee to bestow upon us thy Spirit, that we may grow in the knowledge of thee and ever be comforted by thy faithfulness in the fulfillment of thy Word.

Especially do we acknowledge thy love in bringing us from death unto life by the atoning sufferings and death of Jesus Christ, thy Son, and by the power of his resurrection. Give us, O Father, the spirit of thy love, that, loving thee above all things, we may also love our brethren in deed and in truth. And wheresoe'er any be in want or need, give us compassionate hearts to share what thou hast given us, and grant that they, seeing our love, may live to glorify thee.

We thank thee that in the merits and mercies of Christ our Lord thou hast prepared for us the Great Supper of salvation, and through the preaching of the Gospel hast bidden all to come and partake and to break bread in thy kingdom. We pray that thy church may faithfully bring thy invitation to all nations and that many may respond with ready and willing hearts. Send her messengers forth to invite those in the streets and lanes of the city and those on the highways of life, the poor, the maimed, the halt, and the blind, the weak and the erring, the sorrowful and the troubled, that they may taste of thy Supper and see that thou art merciful and good.

Lord God of hosts, rule over our nation and sanctify all to whom thou hast committed authority. Refine our society by giving it purity of motive, nobleness of purpose, and strength of character. Grant that our destiny may ever be to live in thy trust and obedience.

Bless our homes, that they may be schools of true wisdom and harbors of true love, and that all who abide there may find peace and joy in harmony with thee and one another.

We ask thy special guidance, protection, and comfort for the sick and the sorrowful, the aged and the lonely. Tenderly bestow upon them thy mercy and show them what great things thou hast prepared for thy children.

Hear our prayer, O Father, and if there be aught else we should have asked, grant it unto us for the sake of Jesus Christ, our Savior and Intercessor. Amen.

thiro sunday

O Lord, our God, our Strength and our Joy, who, by delivering Jesus Christ, thine only-begotten Son, to the death of the cross and raising him into glory, didst bring us life and immortality:

We praise thee for thy manifold mercies. In the gifts of our being, our spiritual nature with all its varied capacities, and our physical nature with all its capabilities of activity and enjoyment, thou, having made us in thy image and for thyself, hast been infinitely good, and we thank thee. In the gifts of our human relationships, giving us fathers, brethren, and companions in every walk of life so that we are not alone, thou hast been mercifully kind, and we thank thee. In the gifts of our abode in this rich and beautiful dwelling place of our earthly habitation, and in the heavenly canopy of the infinite starry universe, thou hast been abundantly gracious, and we glorify thee.

But greater than all this goodness is thy mercy in Jesus Christ, in whom thou hast provided for us the full remission of all our sins, however great they may be, the strength to overcome all evil and win the victory in temptation, and the power of an endless life.

Grant, dear Father, that as there is joy in the presence of thine angels over one sinner that repents, we may confess our transgressions before thee, repent of them, hate them, and forsake them. Forgive us our iniquity. Turn thine anger away, and comfort us by thy compassion. Help us to be vigilant in all temptation to sin and in all trials of our faith, that as we steadfastly resist the prince of this world, so may we be preserved from all evil.

Give the riches of grace to thy church, O God, to the end that she may seek the lost, raise the fallen, comfort the broken-hearted, and heal the afflicted. Enable her pastors and missionaries to proclaim with courage and understanding all the words of life which her Lord has given, and to declare thy mighty deeds of judgment and mercy.

Lift high thy banner over all lands and nations, and let it be for an ensign that thou art in the midst of all history, life, and movement, that thou sittest in the councils of nations, that thine eye is in every place beholding the evil and the good, and that according to thy good pleasure thou breakest the bow, cuttest the spear in sunder, and burnest the chariot in the fire. Grant that all eyes may turn unto thee and find thy truth.

Be thou the heavenly Guest in all our homes, and move the hearts of all who dwell there to trust wholly in thee and to have a perfect love toward each other, until the day when thou wilt call us from our earthly homes to ever live together with thee in heaven.

Bless all who are in any need of body or soul, and grant that they may humble themselves under thy mighty hand, so that thou mayest exalt them in due time. Lead them to cast all their burdens on thee, and assure them of thine infinite and understanding care.

O God of all grace, who hast called us unto eternal glory by the mercies of Christ, strengthen, chasten, renew, and perfect us. Hear our prayer in the Name of Jesus, to whom be glory and dominion for ever and ever. Amen.

fourth sunday

O God, King eternal, who didst make the seven stars and Orion and turnest the shadow of earth into the morning of life; who art our light and ion, and our portion forever: We, thy children, seek thee now in prayer, and beseech thee to rest thy hand in benediction upon us.

Bless us, O Lord, with such faith in thy Son Jesus Christ that we may believe in him with all our hearts, and, trusting in his merits, may have the assurance of everlasting life. Bless us, from the fountain of thy love, with the gracious water of life and the washing of regeneration in the Holy Spirit.

Keep us ever within thy care. And as thy glorious creation has been marred by man's sinfulness and lies in travail under the shadow of thy judgment, defend us in all times of danger and save us in every peril. From earthquake and storm, from hatred and war, from tyranny and persecution, from famine and plague, and from corruption and rebellion, deliver us.

Keep us securely within thy grace, O Lord, that, by reason of our sins and frailty, we may never depart from thee. Help us to grow in grace now in the time of our vigor, and in the hour of our death preserve us in the true faith of thy holy Name. Grant that we may have inheritance with all thy children and know the joys of thy adoption in the redemption of our bodies and the resurrection unto life eternal.

Make thy face to shine upon thy church that, through her labor, the light of thy truth may shine in all the world, that thy way may be known upon earth and thy saving health among all nations. Let her watchmen bear thy Name in all godliness and purity, and give her people gladness in thy true service.

Stretch forth thy arm over our land, that thy power and glory may be seen from shore to shore, in the stately halls of government, in the busy precincts of commerce, in the classroom and on the farm, and in the minds and hearts of men of whatever dignity or position in life, that our people may repent and that our land may know that thou art Lord over all and that thou givest thy glory to no other.

Be gracious to all our families, that our children may grow in wisdom and stature and in favor with God and man. To this end give thy Spirit to our parents, that they may be endowed with Christian ideals and live in obedience to Christ's commandments.

Lift up thy countenance, O Lord, upon all who suffer sickness or sorrow, the infirmities of age or the weariness of toil, separation from loved ones or uncertainty in decision, misunderstanding or bitterness, or any other adversity, and grant them thy peace. Show thyself to them as a very present help in time of need, giving them wisdom and understanding, wholeness of mind and body, courage and hope.

These petitions we bring to thee, O Lord, and ask all things for Christ's sake. Amen.

fifth sunday

O Lord of all power and grace, whose eyes are on the righteous and whose ears are open to their cry, hear the prayer of thy people as we come unto thee now in thankfulness for the mercies which thou pourest down upon us anew each day.

We thank thee for the gifts of thy mighty providence and the daily and manifold miracle of making supply for the needs of all creatures, great and small, opening thy hand and giving them their meat in due season. Make us mindful, O Lord, that thou art the Source of the daily bread of all living things, even as thou hast provided them with life, breath, and being.

We praise thee for the gift of thy Son Jesus Christ, whom thou didst send to be the Savior of the world. Grant that we may believe in him with all our hearts, learning from him the great truths of the kingdom to which he bore faithful witness. Help us to obey his commandments with a pure mind, to love him with a true heart, and to serve him with a willing spirit.

We remember before thee, O Lord, our great sinfulness. We repent of our iniquity. Consume us not by thy wrath, but out of thy great compassion forgive us, that we may know the joy of thy salvation and ever live to praise thee.

Grant us thy Holy Spirit, that we may produce the fruits of righteousness. May he endow us with unwavering faith, so that we are ready always to do thy will. Through thy Spirit add to our faith virtue; and to virtue knowledge; and to knowledge temperance; and to temperance patience; and to patience godliness; and to godliness brotherly kindness; and to brotherly kindness love.

Multiply grace, peace, and all spiritual knowledge in thy church. Raise up a ministry that will seek souls for salvation, willing to forsake all selfish concerns and follow thy Son whithersoever he may lead. Give unity of heart and spirit to thy people, O God, and that they may inherit thy blessing and not come under thy judgment, let them manifest the Spirit of Christ in all things. Defend and preserve thy servants wherever they may be suffering for thy Name's sake, and replenish them in faith, strength, and courage by the graces of thy Son.

For the nations of the earth we pray. Subdue terror and tyranny everywhere, and call forth leaders who shall acknowledge that thou art Lord over all the earth. Bless our own land. May it ever follow that which is good and forsake all that is wicked, that our people may prosper in uprightness and integrity.

Hear, O Lord, when we cry unto thee for the afflicted. Grant unto them help in body and soul, and save them for thy mercy's sake. And as we are but pilgrims in the world, guide and uphold us, and bring us all in due time to our heavenly home.

Receive now these petitions in the Name of the Prince of Life, Jesus, our dear Lord. Amen.

sixth sunday

O thou, from whom all goodness flows, holy art thou, and holy is thy Name; heaven and earth are full of thy glory; all the stars, the suns and satellites of space, the marvelous structure of the atom and the mysterious infinity of the universe, all energies and all forces, the sea and the clouds, the thunder and the lightning, the earth and its life, are to thee thy servants, and to us the messengers of thy wonder and might. Yea, O Lord, the firmament showeth thy handiwork; day unto day uttereth speech, and night unto night showeth knowledge; the invisible things of thee are there beheld, even thy eternal power and Godhead.

We thank thee, O Father, that we have a more sure word of light and truth in the Holy Scriptures wherein thou givest us the testimony of our brothers, the holy prophets and apostles. Grant that by thy grace their God may be our God, their love of divine truth our love, and their fellowship with thy people our fellowship.

But most especially do we thank thee for the voice and witness of thy Son Jesus Christ, our Savior.

O thou best Gift of heaven, who in thy birth didst take upon thyself our flesh, and who in thy death didst take upon thyself our sins, give us thy Word and Truth and all the mercies of thy sacrifice, that we, being baptized into thy death, may be raised to newness of life. Enable us by thy power to crucify the lusts of the flesh, to put away all hatred and bitterness, to overcome all sinful habits, and to be born again in the Spirit and ever to live unto thee.

O Spirit of the living God, who hast created the church, by thy gracious power quicken her in faith and life. Grant that her people may bring unto her altars all the fruits of righteousness and show forth the praises of him who has called us out of darkness into his marvelous light.

Give the Light of life, O Lord God, to the nations of the earth, that they may put away sin, acknowledge thy Son Jesus as Lord and Savior, and walk before thee in obedience and faith. Endow our own country with leaders whose consciences are attuned to thy voice and citizens whose wills are fixed on doing thy will.

Bless all who stand in some special need of thy mighty aid. Especially do we entreat thee for our sick and all who may be in bodily or mental anguish. Grant unto them the balm of thy love, and show them what great things thou hast prepared for all who love thee.

O God, Creator, King, and Spirit, help us now in the days of our flesh to lighten by every Christian virtue the place in life to which thou hast called us, and in the time of our death preserve us for thine eternal kingdom, through Jesus Christ, thine only-begotten Son, our Lord. Amen.

TRINITY

seventh sunday

O thou holy and immortal God, who coverest thyself with light as with a garment, and who stretchest out the heavens like a curtain; who makest the clouds thy chariot, and who walkest upon the wings of the wind: In humility of soul we give thee thanks and praise for thy manifold kindness.

We thank thee that thou hast so bountifully given to the world its daily bread, providing the rich earth with its wonders untold, the seed whose powers unfold in abundant harvest with the light and the air, and the dew and the rain to make fruitful the labors of the husbandman.

But we do especially thank thee that in thine ineffable love thou hast provided for our soul's hunger in the gift of the Bread from heaven, Jesus Christ, thy Son. Grant, O Father, that we may believe on him with all our hearts and find the joys and satisfactions of this heavenly Food.

O Lord, we hunger for spiritual knowledge: Give us faith so that, as in the days of his flesh men beheld in him the brightness of thy glory, we may find in him the riches of divine wisdom and heavenly knowledge.

Our souls yearn for truth: Lead us to his heavenly word and doctrine, there to find the great and sublime truths of thy holy will.

We cry for forgiveness and pardon: Turn us to him, who was

bruised for our iniquities and wounded for our transgressions that by his stripes we may be cleansed, healed, and forgiven.

Our souls crave for life: As thine unspeakable gift is eternal life through Jesus Christ our Lord, feed us on this Bread of Immortality, that we may know the power of his resurrection.

O God, grant that we may also find in him the strength we do not find in ourselves: the power to uphold us in the toil and the conflict of this earthly life, and therein to live unto thee, the resolution to do thy will so that we may be thy true and faithful servants, and the will to overcome our sins and yield ourselves to righteousness unto holiness. Nourish us by thy grace that we may find our labor sweet and our work welcome and all our necessities of soul and spirit supplied.

Set watchmen over thy church who shall pray without ceasing for the prosperity of the Gospel in all lands and nations, preach thy holy Word with all boldness, prepare thy people for the time when our Lord Jesus shall return to the earth, and present unto thee in the end a holy and redeemed church.

We have thought of thy loving-kindness to our own country, and we thank thee for the good thou hast given us. Give strength to all the forces of righteousness in our midst, and overthrow all the powers of evil. Be to us ever our Sword and Shield.

Be thou the Helper of all our families. Implant thy Word in the hearts of our children and thy love in our parents, so that they may enjoy now and forever the fruits of holiness.

Free the afflicted from their troubles and bind them to thee, to the end that they may have abundant life, and live to serve and praise thee.

O thou, who seest us, who knowest our frame and rememberest that we are dust, as we go from this holy place, by thy great mercy quicken us in faith, hope, and love, that today and every day we may live as thy children in thy presence; through our Lord Jesus Christ. Amen.

eighth sunday

O heavenly Father, who by thy Son didst create all things that are in heaven and earth, visible and invisible, whether they be thrones or dominions, principalities or powers, giving him authority over all: We thank thee that through him we have received the spirit of adoption, whereby we may truly know thee as our Father, call upon thee in prayer, and be assured that we will be heard as thy children.

Father, for thy church and thy people we pray. Grant unto them ministers and teachers who are counseled and led by thy Spirit, and who earnestly hold forth the Word of life, diligently gather thy children, and teach them all things whatsoever our Lord has commanded. From all false prophets and deceitful guides save them, that they, being knit together in love, may stand fast in one spirit, and with one mind strive together for the faith of the Gospel.

Declare thy glory, O Father, among all nations, and send forth thy messengers to open the eyes of the unbelieving, to turn them from darkness to light, and from the power of Satan unto Christ, that they may receive forgiveness of sins and inheritance with all the children of God. Look with favor upon our own land, that true liberty, perfect justice, and pure morals may prevail in every estate of our society, and that all ungodliness and wicked works may be destroyed.

Father, let thy Spirit descend upon our homes. Let the Word of Christ in all wisdom dwell richly in the children, and grant that all parents may be worthy examples of true Christian virtues. Shelter them in every storm, and preserve them from all evil.

And as thou, dear Father, didst send thy Son, that whosoever believes in him should not perish but have everlasting life, keep us by thy mighty power blameless in the midst of a perverse world, so that we may attain the crown of life. To this end grant that we may be filled with the knowledge of thy will, be fruitful in every good work, and be strengthened in the patience of faith. Help us to mortify the deeds of the flesh and to live in the Spirit, ever setting our affection on the things above.

O Father, from whom all good counsels and just works do proceed, give unto thy children who may be enduring pain, sickness, the threat of disease, mental or spiritual anguish, or any other adversity of the body or soul, such an assurance of thy love and mercy that they may commit themselves wholly into thy care and receive from thee all things needful for their salvation.

Now, heavenly Father, as thou hast bidden us by thy Word to let our requests be made known with thanksgiving in prayer and supplication unto thee, we come to thee in loving gratitude and trust, offering these petitions in the Name of Jesus Christ, our Redeemer. Amen.

ninth sunday

Almighty and everlasting God, who searchest all hearts and knowest all thoughts, whose eyes are in every place, beholding the evil and the good, grant us now, as we approach the throne of thy grace, true humility and penitence. We entreat thee, remember not the sins of our youth or our manifold transgressions, but according unto thy tender mercies, and for the sake of Jesus Christ, thine only-begotten Son, pardon our iniquity.

By the indwelling of thy Holy Spirit, save us from lusting after evil things, from idolatry, from immorality, from unbelief, or other great and shameful sins; and vouchsafe unto us such steadfast faith that in whatsoever trial we must undergo, we may in no wise test thy forbearance by murmuring, complaint, or doubt. Lead us not into temptation, but and if thou dost permit it, strengthen us by thy power to withstand it in the evil day, and by thy providence overrule it, that we may be delivered from the reach of the tempter's arm.

Grant unto us true understanding of thy Word, so that we may be guided in all judgment, and be shown the way that leads to everlasting life. Keep before our eyes the warning and admonition of the Holy Scriptures. Enable us to learn by the examples there set forth what things we ought to do and what things thou hast forbidden and wilt most surely punish; and help us to obey thy commandments with joy.

We thank thee for all thy benefits. Help us to use with faithful stewardship all that thou hast bestowed upon us, being heartily grateful for thine unfailing goodness and deeply conscious that thou wilt call us one day to give an account of our stewardship.

O Lord, remember the covenant thou hast made with thy pilgrim church and with thy people. Provide for them pastors and teachers who shall lead them to the spiritual Rock, Jesus Christ, that they may drink from the living Fountain the pure water of eternal life. Preserve them from all who would beguile them with false words, and keep them from all heresy, schism, or false religion.

Glorify thy Name in all the earth, and send forth men and women to proclaim the Gospel with wisdom, love, and boldness, so that multitudes out of every nation shall call upon thy Name and be saved.

And as righteousness exalts a nation, but sin brings thy reproach, keep our country and people within thy care, that honor and honesty, truth and integrity, may be upheld, and that all lawlessness, wickedness, and rebellion may be put down. Especially do we entreat thy favor upon all who bear responsibility for our government, that they may be endowed with wisdom to govern after thy good pleasure.

Guard and defend our homes, that parents may be kept in the bonds of love and godliness, and may rule their children well, nourishing them in truth and righteousness.

We pray for all who may be ill in body, mind, or spirit, for all who may be in danger of body or soul, for all who may be in anxiety or perplexity, for all who may be suffering some keen disappointment or defeat, be thou present with them in their affliction, show them the way out of all their troubles, and save them for thy mercy's sake.

Heavenly Father, who didst not spare thy Son but freely delivered him up for us all, mercifully grant these and all other acceptable petitions which thou readest in our hearts, in his Name. Amen.

tenth sunday

O God, our God, by whose Spirit all things are ordered in thy kingdom, so that if aught be done, it is thou who hast done it; if aught is given, it is thou who hast given it; or if aught be withheld, it is thou who hast withheld it: Mercifully hear our prayer, and to this end pour out thy Spirit upon us, that we may draw nigh unto thee in the true beauty of holiness.

Grant through thy Holy Spirit that thy Word may come unto thy church, that thy people may hear it from Christ-like teachers with the ears of faith, and, turning to thee in the fullness of love and trust, may know thy will, repent of their transgressions and iniquities, and amend their ways by obedience to thy commandments.

By thy Spirit help thy church to confess unceasingly and proclaim unwaveringly that Jesus is Lord to thy glory, and that he who by his bitter sufferings and death redeemed us from all sin, sits at the right hand of thy power, having authority over all things in heaven and earth, and that he shall reign until all enemies are under his feet.

Give, by thy Spirit, all such diverse spiritual gifts as are necessary to the witness and work of thy church, so that there may ever be abundant wisdom and knowledge, faith and healing, prophecy and miracles, judgment and tongues. May thy light go forth, and may people of every nation, kindred, tribe, or realm learn of thy glory.

Grant by the same Spirit that thy house may ever be a house of prayer for all people. Cleanse it of all unrighteousness, that it may be a fit abode where thine honor dwells, thy Name is hallowed, and thy Word is taught.

Keep the nations of the earth in peace and tranquility, and to this end turn the hearts of men from war and wickedness. Especially do we beseech thee to bless our own land and all who rule over us, that our liberties may be preserved and our laws upheld, that injustice may be suppressed and lawlessness punished. Grant that goodness may be honored and labor enjoyed, that licentiousness may be despised and ease abhorred.

May the words of our Lord Jesus be taught daily in all homes, that both parents and children may grow in grace through the knowledge of him who is the Way, the Truth, and the Life.

Bestow thy favor upon all useful labor in industry and agriculture, education and science, the professions and the arts, that in their advancement thy people may be prospered.

Look in mercy upon the sick and the hurt, those who sorrow or mourn, the handicapped and the infirm, and hear their cry. Let the healthful powers of thy love come to them, so that they may turn to thee in praise and thanksgiving and bless thy holy Name.

These and all other prayers, hear, O Lord, and grant for the sake of Jesus Christ, thy Son, in whom are hid all the treasures of heaven. Amen.

eleventh sunday

O Lord God, whose paths are mercy and truth unto such as keep thy covenant and testimonies, and whose secret is with them that fear thee, incline thine ear to us and hear our prayer, which we bring to thee, not in our own name or righteousness, but in the Name and by the merits of Jesus Christ.

We praise thee for the glorious Gospel of thy grace, whereby, according to thine ancient and faithful promises, thou didst send, in the fullness of times, thy Son, who died for our sins and rose again on the third day, that we through him might be saved.

We thank thee for the apostolic witness of Christ's resurrection and for making known unto us his power and coming, that, though we have not seen him with the eyes of our flesh, yet both loving and believing in him, we may rejoice with joy unspeakable and full of glory and receive the end of our faith, even the salvation of our souls.

Grant that we may ever stand steadfastly therein, repent most earnestly of our sinfulness, turn to thee for thy forgiveness, and be purged of all iniquity. Give us true humility of spirit. Enable us by thy grace to escape the corruption that is in the world through lust. And that we be neither barren nor unfruitful in the service of our Lord Jesus Christ, fill our hearts and kindle in them the fire of thy love.

Bestow the Holy Spirit upon thy church, O Lord, that it may go forth into all the world bearing thy precious Gospel and preaching

Jesus Christ among all nations for the remission of sins and the hope of eternal life. Save thy church from all its enemies, evil workers, and perverters of the truth, that it may know no other Gospel than that which was once delivered.

We pray for our country and beseech thee, by thy mercy, to give us executive, legislative, and judicial leaders who shall give heed to thy commandments, uphold and foster all good, oppose and punish all that is evil, that all our people may live in peace, safety, and honor.

Pour out thy blessings upon our homes. Give mind and will to all parents to train up their children to know, love, and fear thee, to the end that all may live together in peace, kindness, and understanding.

Hear the prayers of all the afflicted, the sorrowful and those who mourn, the needy and the homeless, the wounded and all in pain, the anxious and the despairing, and lead them by thy mercy to a happy issue out of all their adversities.

Deliver us, O God, from every evil, of body or soul, property or character, and at last, when the hour of death shall come, grant us a happy end and take us from this world of sorrow to thyself in heaven.

These and all other things necessary for us, grant unto us, by thine infinite mercy and grace in Jesus Christ, the Bright and Morning Star of our salvation. Amen.

twelfth sunday

O Lord, the Light of thy people, the Salvation of thine inheritance, and the saving Strength of thine Anointed, we thank thee for the gift of thy Word and for the knowledge of thyself which thou by thy hand didst write in our hearts and in all of thy creation when thou didst lay the foundation of all things. We praise thee for the glorious declaration of thy will when thou didst engrave upon tables of stone thy holy and immutable will. But most especially do we give thee thanks for the more glorious revelation of thyself and of thy grace in thy Son Jesus Christ, the Incarnate Word, whom thou didst command us to hear in faith and to obey in love.

Send forth thy Word into our world today. Implant it in the hearts of thy people, that they may be nourished and refreshed by the eternal and living Spring of heavenly vision and understanding, so that they, delivered by thy mercy from the peril of ungodliness, the power of Satan, and the fear of death, may live to serve and praise thee in righteousness and purity forever.

And as thy Word, like a sword of living power, is a discerner of the thoughts and intents of the heart, let it probe us, showing us the evil and the good, that we, thus examined, may amend our ways, forsake our sins and not come under thy judgment.

Let it be for us also a Lamp unto our feet, that our way may be made sure and our path blessed with thine abiding presence, to the end that we may be preserved in every temptation and trial.

Pour out thy Word abundantly upon the multitudes in every nation, that their eyes may be opened and their hearts turned from falsehood and error, idolatry and evil works, and every vain and corrupt practice. Open their ears to hear the words of thy truth, that the day may dawn in their souls as light in a dark place, and that the day star of spiritual knowledge may arise in their hearts.

Let thy Word everywhere consume thine enemies like fire, and, like the hammer that breaks the rock in pieces, let it destroy all oppression, tyranny, and every abominable thing.

Grant that thy Gospel may be published throughout the length and breadth of our land, that all in every place may come to know Jesus Christ as the only Savior and Source of pardon for sins and hope for eternal life.

Let thy Word shine within our homes, that parents and children may dwell together in love, serve one another in kindness, and find increase in joy in this life and that which is to come.

Give the Spirit of Christ richly to all who are sick or are suffering from any adversity of body or spirit, and grant that they may discover that he does all things well, turning our afflictions into divine blessings.

And since we are not sufficient of ourselves to win the victory of life, supply us through the grace of Jesus Christ with the power of thy Spirit, that we may ever be comforted by thy truth and sustained by thy love.

This we pray in the Name of him who gave himself for us that we might ever live through him, even Jesus our Lord. Amen.

thirteenth sunday

Heavenly Father, eternal and almighty God, who through the blood of the everlasting covenant didst bring again from the dead our Lord Jesus Christ: Perfect us in every good work to do thy will, working in us that which is well-pleasing in thy sight.

By thy Holy Spirit work in us a true and living faith in thee and in thy Son whom thou didst send, that in thy manifold goodness and mercy we may be found in him, not having our own righteousness, which is of thy law, but that which is through the righteousness of Christ.

O thou who art the Author of all good counsels and all holy desires, work in us such love toward thee that we, loving thee with all our hearts, may love our neighbor also. Through thy Word and commandments help us in our earthly pilgrimage to do justly, to love mercy, and to walk humbly with thee. Grant that we may ever show compassion to the needy, honor all men, bear the infirmities of the weak, provide for all men things honest, and having fervent charity toward all. Help us never to render evil for evil or railing for railing, but contrariwise blessing, knowing that thereunto thou hast called us, that we should inherit thy blessing.

Work in us such obedience to the example of our Lord Jesus Christ that we may refrain our tongues from evil and our lips that they speak no guile, that we may do good and shun evil, that we may seek peace and follow after it, that we may commit ourselves ever to thee and to thy tender care.

Move, O Lord, thy church with gratitude for all thy blessings, but most especially for the gift of its greatest treasure, the Gospel of our Lord Jesus Christ. Send it forth unto the uttermost parts of the earth to proclaim the good news of his salvation, and prosper it in all its labors. To this end grant unto all in the ministry of the Word a true understanding, to all in the ministry of education a pure knowledge, to all in the ministry of mercy a loving compassion, and to all in the ministry of authority a holy wisdom.

Bless, we pray thee, our nation, that mercy and truth, honor and peace, may everywhere prevail. Give success to all that work for righteousness in our midst, and overthrow all who work iniquity, that we come not under thy reproach and judgment.

In the sanctity of our homes let the Spirit of Jesus Christ come to strengthen all parents, that they may, by excellent example, encourage their children and youth in the practice of virtue, and lead them to usefulness in thy service and in the service of their fellow men.

Let thy benediction rest upon all in every good and useful employment, and grant them contentment and due reward for all their endeavors. Help all men to see that whatsoever they do in word or deed, they are accountable to thee.

Pour out thy mercy upon all who are in trial or adversity, especially those who are suffering for the sake of thy Son Jesus Christ, and save them by thy mighty power, that they may know that thou art the true and only Sovereign, and thy Son the true and only Savior.

Now, dear Father, for his sake forgive us our sins and cleanse us by his Word, giving us the hope and promise through him of life everlasting. In his Name. Amen.

fourteenth sunday

O God, Lord of Hosts, by the great and living way of thy Son Jesus Christ, we enter into thy gates of prayer with thanksgiving and into thy courts with praise.

We thank thee for the declaration of thy glory in all this vast and starry universe, wherein all who will may read of thy infinite power and wisdom. We praise thee that thou hast filled the earth with life and with riches so that man, made in thy image and endowed with great gifts of mind and hand, may, as thou turnest the wheel of the seasons and renewest the face of the earth, harvest the fruit of his toil, find joy in the birth of each day, and rest in the peace of each night.

Most especially we thank thee, O God, for the gift of thine only-begotten Son Jesus Christ, for his perfect revelation of thee and all thy will, for his holy example of true manhood, and for his innocent sufferings and death for our sins, that we through him might receive the remission of our sins, strength to overcome all evil, and, in his resurrection, the gift of everlasting life.

And as thy commandments are a lamp to our feet, and thy Gospel pure light for our path, O Father, we heartily return thanks to thee for thy Word and the gift of thy Holy Spirit, whereby we may read with understanding, learn with a ready mind, and receive, through the patience and comfort of the Scriptures, hope for time and eternity.

Grant that we may ever live in the Spirit so that, led and empowered by him, we may produce the works meet for repentance, despising the bread of wickedness and the wine of violence, and follow righteousness, godliness, faith, and love, and finally in thine everlasting kingdom receive the inheritance that thou hast promised by thy Son.

We pray for thy church: Rule and direct it that it may prosper in the things whereunto thou hast called it. Defend it against all error and confusion, and preserve it in the true faith of thy holy Name. Quicken it by thy grace, that it may show forth thy praises in every good work and bring to thee the sacrifices of contrition and obedience.

Uphold in our land all that are in authority, that in the maintenance of law and order we may lead a quiet and peaceable life and serve thee without hindrance.

Bless our homes and counsel our parents, that thy teachings may not depart from our midst but be continued in the lives of their children. Guide our youth that they may keep their hearts with diligence, and in faith and purity find a happy issue in life.

We pray for all who must walk along the hard and stony path of affliction with sickness, suffering, or peril. Let their way be filled with light that shines more and more brightly unto a perfect day.

These and all the hidden yearnings of our souls, and any other thing we should have sought of thy mercy, grant unto us for the sake of our Lord Jesus, who ever liveth and reigneth with thee and the Holy Spirit, one God, now and forever. Amen.

fifteenth sunday

O God, thou living God, in whose tabernacle of providence the sparrow hath found a house, and the swallow a nest for herself, the fields are arrayed in beauty with good things, and the pastures are clothed with flocks, we draw nigh unto thee in prayer with true and believing hearts.

We give thee thanks and praise for all thy goodness and mercies, but most heartily and earnestly do we glorify thee for the precious gift of thy holy child Jesus, whom thou didst send to deliver us from the due reward of our transgressions, and by whose resurrection thou hast vouchsafed unto us the unfading crown of life.

Grant unto us, O Father, faith in thy power and goodness, that we may ever trust thee for all our daily needs and fulfill the duties of each day without fear and anxiety for the morrow, knowing that thou orderest according to thy Word all things in heaven and earth, and carest for all thy children.

Bestow thy grace upon us so that we seek not the vanities of this world, nor the deceitfulness of riches, but ever set our highest affection and desire on the things that pertain to thy kingdom and to the righteousness which is by faith and obedience. Open our minds to the understanding that our most precious treasure is the unsearchable riches of Christ, our most satisfying food the Bread of Life, and our most glorious dress the garment of heavenly virtues.

Let thy Word dwell in us richly in all wisdom and spiritual understanding, so that in love and in the fulfillment of thy commandment we may assist one another in our trials and infirmities.

And grant that in all our works of mercy we may have special regard for those of the household of faith. Endow thy church and people with the spirit of humility and sympathy, so that the compassion of Christ may shine forth in love and kindness toward the fallen, the wayward, and the heavy laden, and strengthen thy servants everywhere that they may not grow weary in well-doing.

Shed thy light upon the nations, that all the ends of the world may remember and turn unto thee, and that all kindreds and peoples may worship thee. Bless thou also our own land, that thy reverence and truth may prevail in the councils of government and in the halls of commerce, industry, research, and education.

Through all of life's short day, help our families with thy divine benediction and presence. Be with them in sorrow or joy, sickness or health, disappointment or success, and preserve them with thy grace.

Forgive us our sins, and teach us, O Lord, that thou art a God of holiness and power, who in righteousness and mercy rulest the world and governest all men, and that in thee we live and move and have our being. And forasmuch as we can do no good thing without thee, quicken us in body and soul by thy Spirit, that we may sow the works of faith, love, and hope, and reap the blessed, joyful, and abundant life, through Jesus Christ our Savior. Amen.

sixteenth sunday

Almighty God, the Father of our Lord Jesus Christ, from whom thy whole family in heaven and earth is named, we worship thee for thy manifold wisdom, thy mighty works, and thy perfect holiness; but especially do we praise thee for our reconciliation to thee through the sufferings and death of thy dear Son, which thou didst most awesomely purpose in eternity, that we through faith in him might enter with confidence into thy presence and bring to thee our prayers and petitions.

Out of the infinite bounty of thy surpassing goodness grant unto us, who ever stand in need of thy help and mercy, thy spirit and grace. Bestow upon us the intelligence that leads to a due sense of thy majesty and power and the holy fear which is the foundation of all true wisdom. Unfold to us thy overflowing liberality by providing for the wants and necessities of this present life. Let thy mercy descend upon us as the morning dew, giving us life and breath, health and contentment, and deliver us from every kind of danger to body or soul.

But above all we entreat thee to look upon our moral frailty and spiritual weakness, and the evil we have no power to remedy, and by thy Holy Spirit to strengthen us inwardly by the gift of a true faith in Jesus Christ. Grant that he may be Lord of our lives, giving us the conviction of thy pardon and acceptance, moulding our wills to thy will, purifying our emotions, quickening our consciences, and cleansing the springs and principles of our actions by dwelling in our hearts in faith and love.

Let the love of Christ, which exceeds all human knowledge, pervade thy church, that being therein divinely created, it may thereby also flourish, bearing love for all fellow-Christians, compassion for all in need, and forgiveness for all enemies. May it thus show forth the exceeding greatness of thy love, which is as broad as all humanity, as long as eternity, as deep as any human need, and as lofty as the heaven of heavens.

Bestow upon the nations of the earth such knowledge of thy glory, that they may turn to thee, the only God, and thy Son Jesus Christ, and find salvation. Grant also thy favor upon this land, that multitudes within her borders may turn from evil and come to faith and be filled with all thy fullness.

And as thou art able to do exceeding abundantly above all that we can ask or think, according to the power that works in us, increase thy grace to us and enlarge our trust so that we will unfailingly come to thee in prayer with believing hearts beseeching thee for all our wants and needs, but especially for thy mercy and deliverance. Give a special measure of thy power to those who are in sorrow or mourning, to those who are in pain or sickness, to those who may be in temptation or peril, that they may receive thy blessed aid. And although we have deserved thy chastening and correction, help us to receive them with faith, knowing that thereby thou art in love preparing us for that joyful communion with thee which is to be for all eternity.

These things and whatever else we should have sought of thee but did not, we beseech of thee, O God, through our Redeemer and Lord, Jesus Christ. Amen.

seventeenth sunday

O God and Father, loving Creator of all things in heaven and earth, who art over all, the supreme and only Sovereign, who art through all in ruling and sustaining power, and who art in all for the savour of death or life according to thy holy judgments: We bow in prayer before thee and offer unto thee our common supplication.

Impart to us, for the sake of thine only-begotten Son Jesus Christ, pardon for all our sins and deliverance from the just recompense of our transgressions. By thy power rescue us in temptation from the threatening perils of the world, the flesh, and the devil, and protect us from all danger to our souls.

And as we are unable by our own reason or strength to walk worthily in the faith to which thou hast called us, or to bear honorably the Name of Christ, or to render dutifully the obedience which thou dost command, pour out upon us thy Holy Spirit, that we may have those virtues which are pleasing in thy sight. For our stubbornness and self-will, bestow upon us submission to thy will; for our pride and conceit, endow us with lowliness of mind; for our complaining and vengeful spirits, give us the spirit of meekness; for our resentment and anger, grant us patience. Help us by thy grace to bear in love with each other's faults and infirmities, to serve one another in charity and kindness, and to bless those who may seek to harm us.

Look in mercy upon thy church, O God, and grant that it may keep in peace and love the unity which thou dost give and for which our Lord prayed. To this end produce in it an abiding sense of its oneness in faith in Christ, in repentance for sin, in knowledge of thy doctrine, and in obedience to all that revelation which thou didst provide for us in thy Word. May thy church manifest this unity before all the world, that all men in every place may learn of our one and only Lord Jesus Christ, receive his redemption and the gift in him of everlasting life.

Bless our nation, that throughout the length and breadth of the land its people may worship and serve thee in spirit and in truth, and grant it thy counsel and aid, that it may be preserved in peace.

Show thyself the Guardian of all our families, and enable all parents to give wise reproof, spiritual admonition, and a wholesome example to their children, that in obedience to words fitly spoken they may be edified and strengthened for usefulness and service to thee and to all their fellow men.

Set thy healing powers to work in the sick and all the afflicted. Hear their cry and remember them in thy mercy, upholding them by the comforting power of thy Spirit. Show thyself to them a very present help, the Savior of all men and especially them that believe, and increase their trust in thee, through the love of thy Son Jesus Christ, in whose glorious Name we offer these and all other worthy petitions which thou seest in our hearts. Amen.

eighteenth sunday

O Lord God, who art ever faithful, and who hast not failed in one word of all thine exceedingly great and precious promises, we thank thee for the wondrous gift of Jesus Christ thy Son, and for all the promised graces we have received through him: that in the brightness of his glory we have received knowledge of thine own glory; that in the truth, goodness, and tenderness embodied in him we have learned thy will; that in his obedience unto the death of the cross we have been granted cleansing pardon for all our sins; that in his resurrection we have the earnest and the promise of life everlasting; and that in his ascension to the right hand of majesty we have the assurance of his intercession for our every necessity.

Help us that we may so heartily believe and trust in him, and so truly love and serve him, that in all thought, speech, and action we may manifest his Spirit. From the infinite riches of his grace, from the heavenly treasure of his merits, bestow upon us every gift necessary to renew us in spirit, soul, and mind, and fill us with all the fulness of his love. And, that we may become partakers of thy promise in him and be found at his coming worthy to bear the crown of life, increase in us the measure of faith and rebuke our self-trust; deepen our hope and subdue our self-indulgence; enlarge our sympathies and chasten our self-love; and confirm us in his testimony unto our end.

Preserve thy church, dear God, from false or faithless teachers, and keep her obedient and steadfast in all that thou hast made known unto her in the Holy Scriptures. Grant unto her the refreshing of thy Spirit, that in fellowship with Jesus Christ she may proclaim thy truth with living power, preach thy Gospel in all the world, and minister in love to the needs of men everywhere.

Grant unto the nations of the earth peace and tranquility, that their people may live without fear or want. Enlighten them by the rays of thy love, and preserve them from oppression, wrong, and cruelty.

Support our own land in righteousness and overthrow all wickedness. And as there is no abiding strength in material prosperity, preserve us from the decay of moral corruption, and raise up men and women of holy courage and conscience to warn and admonish us. Protect us against every peril from within and without, and give us thy blessing.

Dwell in our homes, O Lord, and let the trust of our families be centered in thee, so that no difficulty, trial, or adversity shall be able to daunt them, or take from them the conviction that thou art their Helper in time of need.

O thou, who wilt ever strengthen the bruised reed, turn the afflictions of the weary and sick into their teachers, and the tears of the troubled and sorrowful into their instructors, that in all their necessities they may learn divine wisdom and knowledge, and thus be led to look unto thee who art the unfailing Spring of all healing and hope.

All these things, and whatsoever else we should have asked, we pray in the Name of him who is thine only-begotten Son and our Lord, Jesus Christ. Amen.

nineteenth sunday

O Lord God, heavenly Father, who art ever in our midst, and who dost never leave or forsake us, we praise and glorify thee for the infinite mercy which thou didst manifest in the unsurpassed gift to us sinners of thy Son Jesus Christ our Lord, who came to put away our sins by the sacrifice of himself upon the cross, that whosoever believes in him should not perish, but have everlasting life. We thank thee, O Father, for thus commending thy love to us, delivering us from the power of sin and death, and opening to us the gate of heaven.

We confess that we are most unworthy sinners, and that we have transgressed more than we can know of thy will and Word. We repent of our evil and pray that thou wilt give us such faith that we may trust utterly in the righteousness of Christ Jesus for our forgiveness. Pardon our iniquity, we beseech thee, and in him cast all our sins into the depths of the sea of oblivion.

Grant that, by thy truth, our minds may be renewed in righteousness and true holiness, that our consciences may be stirred to discern and choose the good, and that every thought, word, and deed may be brought into captivity to the obedience of Christ. Give us the will and the power to walk in thy paths and live in harmony with thy Word. Endow us with grace so that we may be transformed in character, constant in faith, patient in tribulation, and instant in prayer.

Fill thy church with thy Spirit so that it may have a power, a knowledge, and a wisdom that are above all mere human ingenuity and intellect. Give it great moral conviction, a quickened conscience, and an unshakeable sympathy with all that is pure, all that is holy, all that is true, all that is good. Give unto her ministers and teachers the fidelity, courage, and zeal of true prophets, that thy people may be built up in faith and works, rejoice in thy love, endure in patience every trial, and finally enter thy kingdom by way of him who is the heavenly Ladder, even Jesus Christ.

Let the blessings of thy truth and love stream forth upon the nations, and let them receive all thy revelation in repentance and faith, so that they may be delivered from the barrenness of falsehood and the wastes of godlessness, and go unto the house of God in worship and praise.

We pray for our own beloved country. Give us citizens who perceive that the standard of all that is right is not personal advancement or private favor, not public opinion or party platform, but thy holy will. Give us civil servants who are worthy of honor, and leaders in business and labor who are unselfish and far-sighted, and who are guided by the public good and respect for each man's God-given dignity.

Lavish thy grace upon all families, that each home may, by the Christian love and character there lived, be for the children a foretaste of the joy and blessedness of their heavenly home.

For all who are in any sickness, pain, anguish, or suffering, for all who are in any danger from within or without, we pray. Teach them to turn unto thee and wait upon thee for thy mercy; grant unto them hope and a joyous deliverance out of all their trials, and let them walk in thy light all their days.

These things we pray in the Name of Jesus Christ, our Refuge and Hope. Amen.

TRINITY

twentieth sunday

Almighty God, heavenly Father, who, for them that love thee, makest all things work together for good, in the precious Name of thy Son Jesus Christ our Lord, we give thanks unto thee for all things: for thy mercy in times of health, prosperity, and peace, and for thy fatherly chastening in times of adversity and affliction; for thy goodness in the love of family and the companionship of friends, and for thy strengthening help in paths of lowliness and temptation; for thy bounty in knowledge and wisdom, and for light when the way is dark and unknown. But especially do we thank thee for the gift of thy dear Son, by whose death and resurrection thou hast brought us unto thyself and made us meet to receive all thy manifold blessings freely.

Grant, O Father, that we may be filled with thy Holy Spirit, so that we may have understanding of thy Word and will, and power to walk faithfully therein in obedience and love. Enlighten our minds, that we may rescue the fleeting hours of this life from evil and folly by laying hold of every opportunity to do good. Transform our hearts so that we may find joy, not in iniquity, but in worship of thee, communion with our Lord Jesus Christ, and the fellowship of thy people.

Furnish thy church, O Lord, with such grace that she, with robes washed in the blood of the Lamb, may be adorned as a bride for the heavenly Bridegroom, Jesus Christ. Grant unto her a readiness

136

to sacrifice, a zeal for thy cause, and a faithfulness to thy Word, that she may never falter in her holy calling. Give repentance unto thy people, and clothe them with the garments of faith, hope, and love. Send thy servants unto all nations, opening the hearts of all who hear thy Gospel, and crown their labors with success.

Have dominion over all the earth, and bring all rulers to thy obedience, to the end that all tyranny and oppression may be banished, the love of war and the lust for power broken, and the worship of false gods destroyed. Especially do we beseech thy blessing upon our own land. Revive in our midst the esteem of honor, truth, purity, true religion, and the works of faith. And as thou art the Fountain of wisdom, endow our leaders with sound judgment, good counsel, and sure knowledge, so that we may be preserved from all our enemies, both within and without, and live to serve thee and our fellow men in tranquility and concord.

Teach our families to wait upon thee in every necessity, and provide for them in due season all such things as they may need for body or spirit.

Grant that all who are in sickness or sorrow, tribulation or danger, or who have suffered disappointment or injustice, may increase in faith and love, be kept by thy mighty hand, and be delivered out of all their woes.

These things we entreat thee, O God, to vouchsafe unto us in Christ Jesus' Name and for his sake. Amen.

twenty-first sunday

Almighty and everlasting God, who keepest covenant and mercy with thy servants that walk before thee with all their heart, open thine eyes toward this house where thy Name dwelleth, and hearken now unto the prayer of thy people, that we may be confirmed in thy promises and rejoice in thy love.

Enlighten our minds by thy Holy Spirit, that we may ever hear, read, and receive thy Word in reverence and gratitude; and that, as it instructs us in thy glory in the creation of heaven and earth, in thy providence in the governance of all things, and in thine infinite mercy in the gift of thy dear Son Jesus Christ for our salvation, we may believe it with all our hearts and give it free course in our lives.

Enable us thereby to see ourselves as thou seest us, and help us to confess our sinfulness unto thee and repent of our iniquity. Clothe us with thy armor, that we may be strong in thee and, in the power of thy might, may resist the treacherous wiles of Satan, the sly temptations of the world, and the stubborn weakness of our own flesh. Deliver us from the dominion of darkness and preserve us for the eternal kingdom of Christ our Lord.

Grant unto us the spirit of prayer, that in faith we may unceasingly and boldly seek thy blessings for all our needs, bring thee our supplications for loved ones and our intercessions for all men, and trust in thy goodness to fulfill our joy in thy answer for Jesus' sake.

Protect us from all peril by storm or fire, from plague and famine from war and discord, from treachery and rebellion, from luxury and ease, from ignorance and superstition, from painful and sudden death, and from an evil end. And although we have transgressed thy commandments and deserve thy correction, grant us that we may be warned thereby, learn our dependence upon thee, and walk in obedience to all thy will.

Prosper thy church, that it may be maintained in the true faith of thy holy Name, and uphold thy people that they may worship thee with pure hearts and serve thee and all their fellow men in love. Raise up ministers and missionaries who will honor their calling by a godly life, seek the lost with uncommon zeal, and feed thy flock with the Bread of Heaven.

And as the whole world is in thy power, send forth the Sword of the Spirit into all nations, that the wicked may be judged and overthrown and the righteous defended against all their persecutors. Grant that all who rule may have purpose, diligence, and wisdom to strive earnestly for the peace of the world and the health and happiness of mankind.

Bless, we pray thee, our own land. Endow [the President and Congress of the United States of America, the governors and legislatures of the several states, and] all in authority with understanding and integrity, that they may serve according to thy good pleasure. Give thy favor to industry and agriculture, that they may provide for our use the wholesome fruits of their crafts, and increase in education and research such knowledge as will direct our thoughts to thee and to thy majesty.

All these things we pray in the Name of Jesus Christ, thine only-begotten Son, who by his most bitter sufferings and death, and by his most glorious resurrection, has given to us the promise of the life that now is and of that which is to come. Amen.

twenty-second sunday

O God, who in wisdom didst make the world and establish the heavens, we thank thee for our creation, and that in love thou didst fearfully and wonderfully make us in thine image, granting unto us the gift of intelligence and the power of reason; a house for thy Spirit in the temple of our bodies; a spiritual awareness by which our hearts are restless until they rest in thee; a moral nature wherein, enlightened by divine truth, we may perceive the evil and the good, and by thy grace choose the good; and the capacity of faith whereby we may have inwardly the substance of things hoped for and the evidence of things unseen.

Especially do we thank thee for the gift of faith in the revelation of thyself in thy Son Jesus Christ, by whom thou didst commend thy love toward us, and who by thy grace laid down his life, tasting death for every man, that he might bring salvation unto all the world.

Pour out thy Spirit upon us anew each day, that our love for our Lord may richly grow in divine knowledge, spiritual insight, and true discrimination, unto a harvest of goodness and purity for thy praise. Grant by thy Spirit also that we may be ever kindly disposed toward one another in brotherly love, forgiving one another, even as thou hast, for Christ's sake, forgiven us.

Direct and rule thy church in its fellowship in the Gospel, that it may be steadfast in the faith once delivered to it; and defend it against all its enemies, that it may serve thee without fear. And as we have freely received from thee, move us to give freely, liberally, and gladly for thee in the support of all who toil in thy vineyard in our own and in distant lands. Especially do we lift up to thee thy servants who are persecuted for thy Name's sake. Overshadow them with thy power and fill them with thy Spirit, that they, showing thy glory in their faithfulness and love, may turn the hearts of their oppressors. Remove from the midst of thy people all falsehood and error, and grant them truth and godliness.

Go before the nations as a light to relieve the darkness of sin and ignorance, and lead them into the pathways of peace and happiness, to the end that they may love and glorify thee.

Grant health and wisdom to all in our own land who bear authority, so that they may serve in accordance with thy will, and that we may prosper in the things that make for concord and righteousness. Bring to naught all the devices of the wicked and uphold and further all that is good, that we may be saved from thy wrath and be defended by thy mercy.

Implant thy Word in the hearts of all our children, that they may be raised to lives of usefulness to thy church and to their country. Give to all parents thy blessing and grant them understanding and patience.

Watch over the sick, the sorrowing, and the anxious; be their companion in suffering and their help in tribulation. Preserve those who are in any mortal peril of body or soul, and save them by thy gracious providence. And although, on account of our sins, we have merited thy fatherly correction, help us to receive thy visitation in humility and repentance and turn to thee for pardon and peace.

These and all other things of which we have need, we beseech thee to bestow upon us for the sake of Jesus Christ, our Savior. Amen.

twenty-third sunday

O Lord God almighty, who through the greatness of thy power didst create all things in heaven and earth and hast determined the times and the habitations of all nations, divinely instituting all human authority, we acknowledge thy dominion and render unto thee praise and thanksgiving for thy glory.

We thank thee that thou hast crowned the year with thy goodness and covered thy paths with abundance. Thou hast filled the wells with water, and the pastures are clothed with flocks. The plains thou didst spread with grain, and the valleys thou didst adorn with thy bounty. Thou stillest the noise of the seas and renewest the hills with the rain and the snow. Thou fillest the earth with thy riches and rewardest the industry of man. Thou openest thy hand and satisfiest the desire of all who wait upon thee. Great is thy Name, O God, and marvelous is thy mercy.

Most especially do we thank thee that thou didst bring us salvation and quicken the souls of men in the unspeakable gift of thine only-begotten Son, Jesus Christ our Lord, by whose death we have been delivered from the bondage of sin, and by whose resurrection we have been made citizens of thine eternal kingdom. Grant that in our earthly pilgrimage we may ever look unto him who is the Author and Finisher of our faith, follow his holy example in our life and conversation, and set our minds on the heavenly things thou hast provided in him and prepared for our appearance in glory.

Send forth thy Word into all the earth, that thy way may be known, thy saving health among all nations. Let the righteous be glad in thy truth and sing for joy. Scatter thy enemies, and let all that hate thee flee before thee.

Bestow thy blessing on this land, and grant that all who bear the sword of authority may know thy fear and acknowledge thy power, so that justice and mercy, righteousness and peace, may prevail, that all wickedness may be punished and all violence suppressed. Grant that thy people may render honor to the law by their obedience, pay respect to their earthly rulers by their affection and esteem, and pray for them that they may diligently protect life, property, and liberty, and be guided by thy wisdom.

Make thy church alive with the power of the Gospel. To this end pour out thy Holy Spirit upon it, that it may serve thee with fervency and zeal, rejoicing in hope, patient in tribulation, benevolent in heart, continuing instant in prayer.

Teach the youth of the church to count all things but loss for the excellency of the knowledge of Christ Jesus as Lord, and help the children to receive him with joy and gladness.

Give quietness and confidence to all who may be enduring any trial or adversity of body, mind, or spirit, and grant unto them the rewards of faith and trust in thee.

And since our salvation is nearer than when we first believed, help us, O God, to awake out of our sleep, to cast off the works of darkness, and to put on the armor of light, so that when our Lord Jesus Christ shall return, he may, according to his promise, transfigure this frail body and grant it a resplendent form like unto his. In his Name we pray. Amen.

TRINITY

twenty-fourth sunday

O Lord our God, the Rock of our salvation and the Fountain of all truth, who givest food to the hungry and executest judgment for the oppressed, who openest the eyes of the blind and raisest them that are bowed down, who givest habitation to the fatherless and the widow and lovest the righteous: We give thanks unto thee that thou hast delivered us from the power of darkness, redeemed us with the precious blood of Christ, and, raising him from the dead in glory, hast given us the promise of inheritance with all thy people in the heavenly places.

Grant unto us, as we come unto thee in faith and prayer, the indwelling of thy Holy Spirit, that by his gracious influence we may escape the corruption that is in the world through lust and pride and that we may bear the fruit of true goodness. Through thy Word help us to grow in the knowledge of thee and of thy will and in the grace of our Lord Jesus Christ, so that we may walk before thee according to thy good pleasure all the days of our life, steadfast in faith and love, abounding in spiritual understanding and patience, and strengthened for every work of brotherly kindness and charity. Touch our souls with thy power, that we may be revived and healed, and sanctify our hearts that we may thus show forth thy praises.

Stir up thy church, O Lord, to a remembrance of thy everlasting mercies and thy continual presence. Cleanse, strengthen, and govern it, that it may be thy holy people and a light that shines in the darkness. Send forth shepherds to feed the flock who, by their obedience and love, shall be men of God. Put thy Word into their mouths that truth may prevail and righteousness grow amongst us.

Look in compassion upon our world and let thy Gospel come as the breath of life to all nations, that they may turn from their evil ways, repent of their transgressions, idolatries, rebellions, love of pleasure, vanity, and conceit, and turn to thee for forgiveness through Jesus Christ, and be saved.

Judge our own land, that we may mend our ways, obey thy voice, and, walking in the way of thy commandments, be preserved by thy power from all our enemies. Endow our leaders with wisdom and courage to the end that they may execute justice, protect all that is good, and punish all that is evil, so that we may serve thee in peace and safety.

Bless our homes and defend them against all strife and discord. Grant that our children may know and love him who came to give them the abundant life, and give all parents grace to lead them to the feet of the Lord Jesus by the example of their life and conversation.

We implore thy mercy upon all the sick, the sorrowing, and the suffering. Support them in their trials and deliver them by thy goodness, that, being made whole in body and spirit, they may ever trust in the comfort of thy fatherly care.

And as, according to thy promise, the day of the Lord will come as a thief in the night, give us diligence in truth and godliness, that we fail not to attain to thine eternal kingdom through Jesus Christ, our Redeemer. In his holy Name we pray. Amen.

twenty-fifth sunday

O almighty God and heavenly Father, holy and righteous art thou; thy glory fills the universe, and thy power encompasses the world; thy mercy is from everlasting to everlasting, and thy truth endures throughout all generations. Be thou, O Lord, in the midst of thy people, and hear the voice of our supplication.

We thank thee for all thy mercies. Thy kindness is new unto us each day. We praise thee for the light of thy Word, by which thou hast illumined our darkness. We glorify thee for all thy benefits. No good thing hast thou withheld from them that walk uprightly. But most heartily we thank thee for the mighty gift thou didst bestow upon us in Jesus Christ, thy well-beloved Son, who took upon himself the form of a servant and, being found in fashion as a man, humbled himself and became obedient unto death, even the death of the cross, in order that we might receive the remission of our sins and, being absolved, have the assurance of everlasting life, and the certainty of the resurrection of our bodies on the last day.

In this faith, O Lord, take from us the sting of sorrow and the victory of the grave. In this blessed hope in Christ, who is the First-fruits of them that slept, help us to conquer all fear of death and to live in the confidence that because he lives, we shall also live. Make us mindful that as we have borne the image of the earthly, so shall we bear the image of the heavenly. Comfort by this grace and truth all who are bereaved, and wipe all tears from their eyes.

Deliver us from the tribulations of this world, its false Christs and false prophets, its heresies and divisions, its lies and treachery, its wars and oppressions, its fightings and calamities, its bloodshed and pain, and grant that as the days which thou hast appointed us are few and troubled, we may apply our hearts unto thy wisdom, and ever abide under the shadow of thy love and power, where there is refuge from every peril and where no evil can befall us.

Prosper thy church, dear God, in all its endeavors in the work to which thou hast called her. Help her to work diligently while it is day before the night comes. Cleanse thy church of every impure and untrue thing, that she may be without spot and blemish when her Lord shall return.

Stretch forth thy hand over the nations of the earth, rebuke the vain and proud, free the enslaved, defend the persecuted, and bless the obedient, that all may know that thou art God, and that there is none beside thee. Preserve our own country from the corruption of the wicked, that we come not under thy judgment, and save us that we may be used by thee for the healing of the nations. Breathe thy Spirit upon our land that statesmen may be honorable, business and labor leaders unselfish, scientists and educators God-fearing, and our ministers strong in faith.

We entreat thee to look in mercy upon all the sick and any who are stricken in body, mind, or spirit. Manifest thy presence unto them, and heal them according to thy love and their need.

Forgive us our sins for Christ's sake, and give us that peace which passes all understanding, that joy which no man can take from us, and that hope which fades not away.

In the Name which is above every name, Jesus Christ. Amen.

twenty-sixth sunday

Lord God, heavenly Father, of whom and through whom and to whom are all things, to thee be glory forever and ever. We thank thee for all thy blessings: for our creation and all that exists; for the priceless gifts and endowments of body and mind and for thy daily provision for all the necessities of life; for the joys of home, family, and friends and for good government and just laws; for the light of education and the growth of the healing arts; for thy protection in danger and for thy deliverance from all evil; but most heartily do we thank thee for the gift of thy Son Jesus Christ our Lord, by whom thou hast saved us from wrath and appointed us to obtain salvation and eternal life. Grant that we may be filled with his Spirit and produce the fruits of faith, hope, and compassion, so that when he shall come in his glory we may be received into his eternal kingdom.

And as thou wilt then bring to light the hidden things of darkness and make manifest the counsels of all hearts, make manifest to us our exceeding sinfulness and lead us to repentance; cleanse and purify us by thy grace, that we may be absolved from all our sins and preserved from the power of evil; sanctify all our thoughts, utterances, and endeavors, that we may perfectly love and serve thee; and so direct and counsel us that, according to thy good pleasure, we may daily work out our salvation in fear and trembling, and finally, in the day of judgment, be conformed unto the image of thy dear Son.

Open the eyes of thy church to see that Christ the Bridegroom from heaven is nigh and, as there remains a rest for the people of God, to labor with diligence by proclaiming thy Word with all boldness, that multitudes may be saved to the glory of thy holy Name.

Have dominion over all the nations of the earth, and in every land, by thy Word, call, gather, and enlighten a people who may give love and obedience to thee through our Lord Jesus Christ.

Bless our own land. Guide those who are in authority with thy wisdom, that they may rule with humility, serve with uprightness, lead with vision, and plan with intelligence; and grant that freedom, charity, and unity may dwell among us.

Defend our homes from the corrupting influences of the world, the devil, and our own flesh. Keep our parents in the faith, each one loving and honoring the other, and our children in affectionate obedience, each one growing in grace and favor with thee.

We pray for all sorts and conditions of men, but especially for the afflicted. Lift up the weary and the wounded, touch the sick and the diseased, strengthen the aged and the infirm, give hope to the depressed and anxious, guard the imperiled and oppressed; and by thy mighty power give them in Christ Jesus light for their darkness and joy for their sadness.

And, now, O God, who wilt once more shake the heavens and the earth, but who hast given us a kingdom which cannot be moved, grant unto us steadfastness and patience, that, when thy Son shall appear, and all his holy angels with him, we may be clothed with his righteousness and inherit the heavenly city which abides forever. In his exalted Name we pray. Amen.

the last sunday

O God, who hast saved us and called us with a holy calling, not according to our works, but according unto thine own purpose and grace given unto us in Christ Jesus before the world began, we thank thee for the abundance of thy mercies, but especially for the gift of thy Son, in whom, through his sufferings and cross, thou hast abolished death and, through his resurrection, brought life and immortality to light.

Grant that by thy grace we may ever continue in the things we have learned through thy Word, and of which we have been assured by thy Holy Spirit, so that, being wise unto salvation through faith in the Lord Jesus, we may receive on the day of his coming the crown of righteousness which he has laid up for us and for all who love his appearing. To this end save us from following after perversions and denials of his truth, and from giving heed to lies, deceptions, and vain philosophies.

And as, in his coming in power, he shall judge all the living and the dead, help us to walk each day in the way of thy commandments, to follow peace and holiness with all men, to endure in meekness for thy Name's sake such pain and adversity as we are called upon to bear, to be instant in prayer that we enter not into temptation, to behold the signs of the times, and to look for the new heavens and earth which the redeemed of the Lord shall inherit in everlasting joy and gladness.

Deliver us from every evil work, from all ungodliness, and from worldly lusts; from the proud and disobedient, from corrupt and reprobate men, from the foolish and pleasure-seeking.

Give strength to thy church, that with fervent spirit it may fight the good fight of faith. Raise up a faithful ministry who know Christ in sincerity and truth, and whom Christ will know and own upon his return. Call forth messengers who will endure hardness as good soldiers in carrying his Gospel to all lands. Prosper the schools of the church, that young men and young women may be prepared to serve thee and their fellow men in every useful and honorable vocation. Give thy blessing to the church's institutions of mercy, and grant thine aid to all who labor therein. Bestow heavenly grace upon our parents, that they may teach their children the way of life in Christ Jesus; and keep the young ever faithful in word and deed.

Govern the nations upon earth, and plead thine own cause amongst the multitudes, that they may be turned from their darkness to thy light, and from sin to righteousness. Be thou the Shield of our land. Look upon us in mercy, and make us repentant for our wickedness, immorality, and materialism. Subdue all evil in our midst, and let thy Word flourish, so that truth and holiness may prevail.

Hear the cry of the afflicted and give them thy compassionate aid. Make straight paths for them, strengthening the weak, upholding the feeble, and healing the sick. Enlighten them so that they despise not their chastenings but, receiving them in trust and confidence, bring forth the healthful fruits of righteousness and joy.

Preserve us all in steadfast faith, looking for that blessed hope and glorious appearing of our Lord Jesus Christ, who in his coming will manifest himself as the blessed and only Potentate, the King of kings, and Lord of lords; to whom be honor and power everlasting. Amen.

APOSTLE

ST. ANDREW

November 30

O Lord, King of heaven and earth, the only wise God, to whom be all honor and glory, we thank thee for all thy manifold mercies, but chiefly for the gift of thy Son Jesus Christ, whom thou didst send to declare thy Word and to manifest thy love by taking upon himself the likeness of sinful flesh and becoming obedient unto death: Grant us the inspiration of thy Holy Spirit that with one heart and one soul we may come unto thee now in prayer.

We are especially mindful this day of thy great goodness in the calling and ministry of thy blessed Apostle Andrew, who by the effectual working of thy power gave ready acceptance to the Gospel of our Lord Jesus Christ, followed him steadfastly in faith and obedience, forsook all worldly advantage, and served him with glad heart as a fisher of men.

Give unto us, O Father, a like faith, knowledge, and zeal. Let thy Spirit and Word come unto us. Grant that we may drink deeply of the Fountain of Living Water so that there may be in us wells springing up into everlasting life. Help us to love, obey, and serve thy Son with all our hearts, and in joy to lead others to him who is the Salvation of the world.

And as thou wilt have all men to be saved and to come to the knowledge of the truth, stir up thy church, O Lord, that she may send forth to the far corners of the earth workers who are wholly dedicated to the sowing of thy Word and the gathering of thy harvest, and grant that she may ardently pray thy blessing upon their labors and liberally give of her substance for their maintenance and support.

We beseech thy blessing upon all in authority in every nation: By thy Spirit enable them to rule with wisdom and mercy so that men everywhere may lead a quiet and peaceable life in all godliness and honesty and that thy people may serve and worship thee in the Name of Jesus without fear of persecution or oppression.

Send forth into our land the healthful spirit of thy truth, that multitudes now in darkness may renounce the works of wickedness and come to the joy of faith and hope in thy Son. Open our eyes to see that thou alone art our Shield and Buckler and that thou dost continually overshadow us with thy power.

Behold the needs and trials in our homes; forgive the sins of thy people, and turn their hearts into the ways of kindness, understanding, self-discipline, patience, and purity. Let thy holy angel have charge over our children, and grant unto the parents a spirit of thanksgiving, prayerfulness, and contentment.

Like gentle dew from heaven let thy loving-kindness fall upon the sick, the hurt, and the wounded, and deliver them out of all their afflictions. Strengthen those in temptation or trial, and protect all who are in danger.

We call upon thee, O God, and pray that thou wouldst hear and grant these and such unspoken petitions as are according to thy will, for the sake of thy dear Son, Jesus Christ, our Redeemer. Amen.

st. thomas

December 21

O God, heavenly Father, in whose presence is the fullness of joy and at whose right hand is gladness for the upright in heart, we come to thee in humility and trust and beseech thee to grant unto us thy Holy Spirit, so that whatsoever we, thy people, shall ask will be acceptable in thy sight.

For the mighty redemption thou hast provided for all mankind through the precious blood of Christ, we praise thee, and we magnify thy Name that thou didst raise him from the dead so that we who have borne mortality may be clothed with immortality. Grant unto us such faith in his resurrection and in the testimony of those whom thou didst make eyewitnesses to his glory and power of life that we may in no wise doubt, but firmly believe, to the saving of our souls and the souls of all who trust in him.

We give thee special thanks this day, O God, for the calling of the Apostle Thomas, for his overcoming of disbelief, for his confession of the lordship and deity of Jesus, and for his ordination into a ministry of sacrifice, suffering, and martyrdom for thy Name's sake. Sanctify us also by thy truth, and show us the grace and glory in thy well-beloved Son, that we may exalt him in our hearts and serve him with willing minds. Help us to continue in the doctrine of thy blessed apostles, so that we may not depart from the faith once delivered to the saints, and that, by word and deed, we may daily confess that Jesus Christ is Lord and Savior.

Give to thy church, O Lord, the mind and unity of the Spirit, that nothing be done through strife or vainglory, but that all things may be accomplished in the love of Christ and in obedience to his Word. Let a holy zeal come upon her, that she may fervently seek the lost, diligently instruct them in all thy knowledge, and prayerfully lead them to godliness and true holiness. Raise up pastors and teachers who shall labor for thee and rightly divide the word of truth for thy people; and send to every nation, tribe, and tongue missionaries endowed with understanding of thy will and compassion for the multitudes.

Build up the body of Christ in our own land, and prosper thy cause to the end that faith may be increased, the love of righteousness abound, and every good work advanced. Preserve our homes in purity and love and shelter them continually under the shadow of thy providence. Guide all children into paths of useful and honorable service and virtuous living. Watch over all who are in danger of body or peril of soul, and by thy mighty power protect them. Draw near to the sick, the suffering, and the infirm, and lead them to the pleasant pastures of confidence and the still waters of contentment.

Forgive us our sins and grant unto us the new birth and life in thy Word. Help and save us for thy mercy's sake.

These things we entreat thee in the Name of Jesus Christ, whom not having seen, we love; in whom, though now we see him not, yet believing, we rejoice with joy unspeakable and full of glory. Amen.

conversion of st. paul

January 25

O Lord God almighty, who dwellest in the light which no man can approach, whom no man has seen, nor can see, to whom be honor and power everlasting, we offer unto thee praise and thanksgiving for thy love and mercies.

We bless thee for the gift of thy dear Son Jesus Christ, who gave himself for our sins, that he might deliver us from this evil world, according to thy will, and present us faultless before the presence of thy glory. We sanctify thee for this covenant of thy grace, and that thou hast called, inspired, ordained, and sent forth prophets and apostles to make known the mystery of thy will by the preaching of the Word of thy truth and the Gospel of salvation, so that all who in faith call upon thy Name may receive the Holy Ghost, the remission of sins, and the promise of everlasting life.

We remember on this day especially the mighty grace which turned the heart of a great enemy of our Lord Jesus Christ, brought him from darkness to light, and from the power of Satan to faith in thy Son. By the richness of thy love thou didst make him a chosen vessel to witness to Jews and Gentiles, kings and commoners, philosophers and tradesmen, and the great and the small of the unsearchable treasures in Christ and of the love which passes knowledge. For the conversion of the Apostle Paul by the visitation of our Lord Jesus Christ we thank thee.

Grant, O God of all grace, repentance and faith to all who deny the sonship and redemption of Christ, who oppose thy revelation in him, and who resist the testimony of thy Holy Spirit, so that thy Name may be glorified. May the multitudes who are without hope, without God, and afar off be brought nigh unto thee in Christ Jesus.

Endow us who are in thy house this day with such light that we may know thy will and walk in obedience thereto. Help us to discover the true service to which thou dost call us, and enable us to fulfill the same with singleness of heart. Direct us to this end, and perfect us in every work that is well-pleasing in thy sight.

Fill thy church with thy Holy Spirit that she may produce the fruits of righteousness, experience the fellowship of Christ's suffering, and, being made in conformity to his death, stand fast in one spirit, with one mind striving together for the faith of the Gospel, and in no wise be dismayed by her adversaries. Call forth pastors and missionaries who shall count all things but loss for the surpassing knowledge of Christ, and help us to hearken earnestly to their words, that we may zealously seek the prize of thy high calling in him.

Bless and strengthen our families, and vouchsafe that they may set their minds upon thee and all the things that are true, honest, just, and pure, and so be preserved in peace, love, and all goodness.

Clothe our sick and suffering, and all who are in any pain or peril, with the garment of thine infinite kindness, leading them to pray always with all faith and perseverance. Show them what great things thou canst and wilt do for all who bear thy Name and cry unto thee in sincerity and truth.

All these things we pray, not in our own name or righteousness, but in the name and righteousness of Christ, who died for us, that, whether we wake or sleep, we may live together with him. Amen.

PRESENTATION OF OUR LORD

February 2

O Lord God, who didst send forth thy Son Jesus to be born of woman and to be made under the law so that he might redeem us who are subject to thy law, we thank thee that in his presentation in the temple thou didst reveal him as our Wisdom, Righteousness, Salvation, and Sanctification.

Grant that in Mary's first-born child we may behold our Lord and Savior, the Builder of the more glorious and perfect temple not made with hands, eternal in the heavens, wherein he entered by a new and living way through the veil of his flesh. Make us mindful of all that he suffered for us in the lowliness of his birth, the temptations he endured, and the cross he bore. Illumine our souls with the example of his gracious humility and loving submission to thy will, and as thou didst give thy Son to be the Light of the world, let his life-giving words be shed abroad in our hearts, that we may be delivered from the power of darkness, live in the glorious liberty of the children of God, and have the light of life. Give us understanding in his truth, the will to walk steadfastly therein, and to be filled with all the fruits of righteousness, peace, and holiness, without which no man may see thee.

O God, give us the spirit of thanksgiving for thine infinite goodness in the gift of thy holy Child Jesus, and for the door to thy grace and mercy opened to us through him.

Let the Desire of all nations come to them in power and grace, that they may seek those things which are above and render glory to thee alone. Visit them with thy quickening Spirit and enable them to receive the Gospel in faith, to believe it in sincerity, and to continue therein with joy.

Look with thy most tender favor upon our land, and let justice and mercy, righteousness and peace, truth and honor everywhere prevail. Uphold all those to whom thou hast given authority, that they may have wisdom to perform their duties in thy fear. Prosper all honest labor and advance every true calling.

Bless all the families of the church, that the young may be brought unto thee and come to know the Lord Jesus as their Shepherd. Embrace our parents within the arms of thy strengthening love, that they may always do such things as please thee.

And as it is thy good pleasure to be the Consolation of the sorrowful and the Deliverer of all those that are bowed down in adversity, lead the afflicted into the sanctuaries of prayer, there to behold the beauty and health of thy compassionate care, to seek thy mercy, and to receive thine omnipotent aid.

And when our last hour shall come, let us depart in peace according to thy Word, and grant us habitation with thee and all thy saints in glory everlasting, through Jesus Christ, thy Son our Lord, who ever lives and reigns with thee and with the Holy Ghost, one God. Amen.

st. matthias

February 24

O Father, Lord of heaven and earth, who hast made known thy glory in the creation of all things and whose handiwork declares thy wisdom and power, we thank thee for the perfect manifestation of thy love in the gift of thine only-begotten Son Jesus Christ, whom thou didst send to be the propitiation for our sins, and not for ours only but for all who by faith receive him as Lord and Savior.

We praise thee for his sinless life, his perfect truth, and his innocent sufferings and death, and we beseech thee to grant us such faith in him and such obedience to his revelation of thy Word and will that we may be accounted worthy to be numbered among his disciples and receive a share in the inheritance which thou hast promised to all who love and serve him.

We especially bless and hallow thy Name this day for the providence which ordained the blessed Matthias to the office of apostle and endowed him with grace to witness to our Lord's Passion and resurrection, to proclaim thy Word with truth and power, and to feed the church with heavenly doctrine.

O God of all grace, who hast called us unto eternal glory by Christ Jesus, endow us with thy Holy Spirit, that we may ever be preserved against all the assaults of the devil, the world, and our own flesh, and that we may not fail to attain to the redemption which he has won for us. Deliver us from weakness in temptation and from every trial that would imperil our souls. Strengthen and uphold us, and grant that we may steadfastly commit the keeping of our souls unto thee.

Look in mercy upon thy church, O Lord, and quicken its spirit, deepen its love, and heal its divisions. Raise up watchmen who shall not fail to counsel, admonish, and warn with grace and truth, so that thy people may sanctify thee in their hearts, honor thee with their substance, and seek those things which are above. Comfort thy church by thy presence and establish it in every sound word and work.

Send thy light unto the nations of the earth, that in every place men may humble themselves under thy mighty hand, acknowledge that there is none other name under heaven than Jesus whereby they may be saved, and turn to him in repentance. Bless our land, that brotherly kindness and charity may rule in the hearts of this people and that virtue and righteousness may increase.

We pray for all sorts and conditions of men. Grant safety to all travelers and deliverance to all who are in any danger. Prosper all who in their callings render true service, and uphold and further all who labor for peace and good-will among men. Watch over all children and youth, that they may be kept from harm in body and soul. Protect us from war and preserve us from treachery and rebellion. Save us from storm and fire, from pestilence and hunger. By thy mercy heal the sick and grant relief to those in pain and, with the sword of thy power, rescue the oppressed and the persecuted.

And as there is but a step between us and death, help us to watch in all godliness and prayer, so that when thou callest us from this world, we may enter into the joy of our heavenly home.

These things we, thy people, pray, O Lord, with one mind and one spirit in the Name of thy Son Jesus Christ our Lord. Amen.

the annunciation

March 25

O Lord God, who in the creation of the world didst command the light to shine out of darkness, we thank thee that thou didst shine also in the darkness of our hearts with the light of the knowledge of thy glory in the face of Jesus Christ.

We bless thee for his coming, that thou didst send him in the likeness of sinful flesh to condemn sin in the flesh, to fulfill for us the righteousness of the law by his innocent sufferings and death, and to be raised from the dead, that he might quicken our mortal bodies by the indwelling of his Spirit.

We give thee thanks that thou didst ordain thy Son Jesus to an exalted inheritance, far above all principalities and powers, giving him a Name which is above every name, and granting him dominion over all the earth, the throne over all thy people, and a kingdom of which there shall be no end.

Especially, O God, this day do we praise thee for thy gracious visitation by thy holy angel to the Virgin Mary, for the anointing of one so pure and holy to be the earthen vessel to bear so great a treasure, and for the overshadowing of her by the power of thy Holy Spirit, that by her thy Son might become incarnate.

Grant unto us also the readiness to obey thy commandments, live according to thy Word, and submit to thy will, that we may be blessed with thy favor and receive thy mercy. Teach us to rejoice in thy goodness, and to seek the things that are true, pure, and just.

Help us to cast all our care upon thee and to stand in thy strength, so that we may be delivered from distress, despair, and perplexity. Forgive us our sins and save us in all temptation. Grant unto us the spirit of repentance, the gift of faith, and the confidence that thou wilt supply all our need by the riches of thy grace in Christ Jesus.

Establish thy church and the truth of thy Gospel throughout the earth and raise up faithful messengers who shall declare thy Name with power and compassion. Increase the faith and love of thy people, that they may be effectual witnesses of the redeeming grace of the Lord Jesus Christ.

Let him reign over the nations of the earth and, by the inspiration of thy Holy Spirit, let them acknowledge him as King of kings and Lord of lords. Make manifest thy mighty providence in our own land. Let righteousness and brotherliness here prosper, and overthrow all wickedness and evil.

Abide with our families and grant unto them such confidence in thy presence that they may in no wise be anxious, but ever turn to thee in faith and prayer.

And as our light afflictions are but for a moment and work for us a far more exceeding and eternal weight of glory, grant unto all who face adversity or peril, trial or temptation, the renewal of thy Spirit.

These and all other things needful for us grant unto us, O God, for the sake of him, even thy Son Jesus, before whom all must appear when he comes to judge the earth in righteousness. Amen.

EVANGELIST

ST. MARK
April 25

O God, Creator almighty, who dwellest in light unapproachable, whom no man has seen or can see, but whose providence overshadows all who love thy truth and do thy will: We give thanks unto thee that thou hast made thyself known through thy mighty acts and the Word given unto the prophets and apostles.

But especially do we offer unto thee our most heartfelt thanks for the revelation of thy love and grace in the person of thy holy Child Jesus. We praise thee for the surpassing mercy of his Passion and cross, whereby he who was without sin became sin for us, that he might atone for our iniquity, and open for us the gates of heaven and bring us to immortal glory.

We hallow thy Name also that thou, through the inspiration of thy Spirit, hast preserved unto us in the Scriptures of the holy Evangelists the saving knowledge of our Lord Jesus Christ, so that we may believe that he is the Son of the living God, and that we may have life through his Name.

Especially do we thank thee this day for the life and labors of thy servant Mark. Grant, heavenly Father, that we may so read his Gospel that we by thy grace may learn therein what things we ought to know, believe, and do, and give heed thereto by a sincere faith and obedient life. Help us to find refreshment from this pure fountain of living water, to be cleansed through the Word thou hast caused to be spoken unto us, and to bring forth the abiding fruits of righteousness and peace.

Strengthen thy church for the work unto which thou hast called her. Let the Word of Christ abide in her richly in all wisdom and spiritual understanding, and enable her to keep the commandments of her Lord faithfully, so that she may continue in his love, and that her joy may be full. Purge her of all that is unclean, impure, and heretical. Call forth from her midst men and women who shall find favor in thy sight, and send them to the uttermost parts of the earth to declare with courage and love the glory of Christ.

Let thy light shine in the darkness of the nations, that they may turn to thee, repent of their sins, seek peace and brotherliness, and forsake all wickedness and unholy ambition. Give grace to the leaders of our country that they may discharge their duties in thy fear, and prosper us in all the things which insure a quiet and peaceable land.

And as thy Word instructs us to be kind to one another, tenderhearted and forgiving, endow our families with these virtues, for the sake of Jesus Christ.

For all who are in want and need we pray; supply them by the riches of thy Son. For the sorrowing and the bereaved we beseech the matchless comfort of thy promises; and for those in pain or peril we entreat thy mighty deliverance and protection.

Continue us, O God, in sound doctrine, and deliver us from the enemies of thy truth, until we all come in the unity of faith and love to thy heavenly kingdom, through Jesus Christ our Savior, in whose exalted Name we pray all these things, and who ever lives and reigns with thee and the Holy Ghost, one God, in the world without end. Amen.

APOSTLES

st. philip and st. james

May 1

Heavenly Father, gracious and ever-living God, who, in thy compassion upon all mankind, didst freely deliver thy well-beloved Son to the humiliation of the flesh and the death of the cross, so that as many as believe on him should not come under condemnation, but have everlasting life: We praise thee for thy goodness and mercy.

Grant that we may so receive him in repentance and faith, that we may be absolved of all our sins, be preserved against the power of the devil, the love of the world, and the lusts of the flesh, and, following after righteousness and holiness, receive inheritance in thine eternal kingdom.

We give thee this day praise and thanks especially for thy servants Philip and James, whom thou didst choose to be instructed in the truth of Christ and to be witnesses of his temptations and glory, and whom thou didst send forth in the power of thy Spirit to speak faithfully and teach diligently all the words that pertain to this life and the life which is to come.

Bless, we pray thee, thy church, that her pastors and teachers may expound more perfectly the truth of thy holy Word and build up thy people in all thy will and grace, and grant that all may receive their words with true hearts, grow in the knowledge of and obedience to our Savior, and produce the fruits thereof by steadfast continuance in his love and doctrine. Give thy favor to all her works of mercy and thy blessing to all her schools, that in faithfulness to their calling they may reverently hold forth the Word of life to all in their care, lead them to the Source of all true wisdom and comfort, and guide them in rendering unto thee a pure and acceptable service.

And as thou hast made of one blood all nations of men to dwell on the face of the earth, and hast determined the times and bounds of their habitation, cause thy glory to dwell among them, that they may know thee as Creator and Sovereign of the universe, as Judge of the nations, and as Redeemer of all mankind. Grant that, walking in thy light, they may live together in peace and concord.

Lift up thy countenance upon our own land and heal us of all iniquity. Turn us from the ways of wickedness, from the pride of life and the lust of the flesh, from pernicious doctrines and the praise of evil men, and humble us before thee in contrition and repentance. Raise up among us civil servants who will seek to do thy will with courage and constancy. Give us the spirit of obedience to sound ordinances and, by thy power, overthrow all our enemies within and without.

Shelter in the arms of thy love all families, that they may be preserved from the evil of our times. Help our parents to live according to thy good pleasure, and keep our children in the grace of Christ.

Unto all who are in affliction and adversity, in pain or suffering, or who may be enduring the infirmities of age, the perils of occupation or travel, the persecutions of men, the calamities of the elements, or who are suffering for thy Name's sake, grant such deliverance that they may live to praise thee and by word and deed show forth thy loving-kindness.

These and whatsoever other things thou seest we have need of, vouchsafe unto us for the sake of him who is the Way, the Truth, and the Life, even Jesus Christ, our Lord and Savior. Amen.

THE NATIVITY OF

St. John, the Baptist

June 24

O Lord God, heavenly Father, who, since the world began, hast spoken unto us by the mouth of thy holy prophets and given unto us exceeding great and precious promises, we thank thee that thou hast been faithful in all thy covenant, and didst visit and redeem thy people by raising up in the house of David a Prince and Savior, even Jesus Christ, to give them remission of sins, deliverance from the power of evil, and the hope of everlasting life.

We praise thee especially this day that thou didst prepare the way of our Lord by the word of thy prophet and messenger John the Baptist, whom thou didst ordain as a preacher of repentance; and that by his voice, as of one crying in the wilderness, thou didst give knowledge of salvation unto thy people, light to them that sit in darkness and in the shadow of death, and counsel to guide their feet into the way of peace.

Grant us, we beseech thee, the gift of thy Holy Spirit, that we may receive in faith the testimony of those who beheld the divine glory of the Lord Jesus Christ and who, without wavering, bore witness to his grace and truth even unto death, to the end that according to thy glorious power we might be strengthened against all temptation, be filled with the knowledge of thy will, be fruitful in every good work, and be made worthy to be partakers of the inheritance of the saints in light.

Rule and govern thy church upon earth, O Lord, that all who

preach therein may do so with fearlessness and fidelity, that all who teach therein may have wisdom and grace, and that all who in any way serve therein may hold the faith in a pure conscience and seek those things which pertain to thine eternal kingdom. Bestow upon them the mind of Christ and deliver them from error and schism, lukewarmness and hypocrisy.

We pray for the nations. Turn them to the Lamb that takes away the sins of the world. Incline the hearts of the multitudes to the reception of his truth, and deliver them from the tyrannies of force, falsehood, and fear. Give them knowledge of thy salvation and save them from the works of evil.

Preserve our own land in righteousness and peace, and to this end give diligence and devotion to all who hold authority, that they may administer our laws in accordance with thy will, encourage obedience thereto, and punish all wickedness.

Let thy benediction rest upon our homes. Nourish our children in the words of faith and good doctrine, and keep all parents in the way of godliness, so that they may be patterns of love and purity for their children.

Remember the afflicted, and touch them with the healing power of thy presence. Manifest thyself as a very present help in time of trouble, their Strength and their Shield.

And as thou hast appointed a day when thy Son shall return to judge the world in righteousness, keep us by thy grace and mercy in continual fellowship with thee and with all who look for his appearing.

These petitions we entreat thee to grant, and such other things as thou seest we need, in the Name and for the sake of Jesus Christ, our Lord. Amen.

st. peter and st. paul

June 29

O God our Father, who didst establish thy household, the church, upon the foundation of the prophets and apostles, Jesus Christ thy Son being the chief cornerstone, we thank thee for the most glorious ministry thou didst give unto thy servants Peter and Paul, whom thou didst deliver from darkness into thine ineffable light, and who, under the guidance of thy Spirit, renounced the works of the law for the righteousness which is by faith in Christ, expounded thy Word in the fullness of truth, and preached Christ crucified as the only Savior of men.

We praise thee that thou didst call and ordain them for the perfecting of the saints, for the work of the ministry, and for the edifying of the body of Christ. We thank thee that they wearied not in their mighty labors, but, empowered and strengthened by thee, when troubled were not distressed, when perplexed were not in despair, when persecuted were not forsaken, when cast down were not destroyed, so that, bearing in their bodies the marks of Christ's death, they also made manifest his life and the victory which overcomes the world.

Grant unto us, O God, the same faith, that, continuing steadfastly in their doctrine, preserved for us in the Holy Scriptures, we may be delivered from sin's gall of bitterness and the bondage to death and the devil, and be raised to newness of life in the love, grace, and power of Christ. Increase that faith day by day in our hearts; give us the assurance that nothing in this world can separate us from thy mercy in him; and help us so to walk in obedience to his commandments that, whether present or absent in the flesh, we may be accepted of him.

Uphold and defend thy church, the steward of thy mysteries, that it may ever be found faithful. Deliver it from the hands of its enemies, and keep it from lukewarmness and indifference. Save it from the temptations that attend prosperity and ease. Make it to hunger and thirst after righteousness. Give it deep concern for all thy children everywhere and unceasing prayerfulness for those of the brethren who are oppressed and persecuted.

Let thy servants go forth to prophesy to the nations, and open doors for them in every land, that thy Name may be hallowed and thy kingdom come.

Be pleased to visit our country with thy mercy, and let the light of thy Word shine forth into all our homes, so that we may obey thy voice and amend our ways and not come under thy judgments. Destroy all works of iniquity, and prosper the endeavors of those who labor for righteousness' sake.

And as thou hast called upon thy people to lift up with holy hands the needs and wants of all men, we pray for all who are overshadowed with the clouds of suffering, sorrow, or peril, and beseech thee to grant unto them thy merciful aid, that they may be delivered from all evil and live to sing thy praise.

Now unto him who, with his apostles, was appointed unto death and made a spectacle unto the world and before men and angels, but whom thou didst exalt by thy power to sit in heavenly places, even thy Son Jesus Christ our Lord, to him be glory and dominion and majesty forever and ever. Amen.

the visitation

July 2

Almighty and all-knowing God, whose goodness never fails and whose mercy is from everlasting to everlasting upon all them that fear thee, we lift up our hearts unto thee in prayer and thanksgiving, and beseech thee to hearken unto the voice of thy people.

We bless and honor thee that thou didst bestow upon us the gift of thine only-begotten Son Jesus Christ, and didst wonderfully promise that whosoever believes on him should not perish but have eternal life. We entreat thee that thou wouldst give us such faith in him, his mighty works and words, his innocent sufferings and death, and his glorious resurrection and ascension, that we may receive the remission of our sins, be delivered from the bondage of Satan, and finally, in fellowship with all thy saints, receive the laurel of victory.

Especially do we thank thee, O Lord, for the pure and holy Elizabeth and Mary, thy chosen handmaidens in the marvelous salvation which thou didst prepare before the face of all peoples. We praise thee for the graces that were bestowed upon them: lowliness and quietness of spirit, faith and heartfelt trust, sincere love and obedience; and we entreat thee that thou wouldst vouchsafe unto us in like measure the fullness of the Holy Ghost, that we may rejoice evermore in thy faithfulness, and that our souls may magnify thy glory.

To this end grant that thy Word may have free course in our lives, take possession of our affections, and direct and rule all our thoughts, so that we may abound in all faith, utterance, and knowledge, and serve thee with pure hearts and willing minds.

And as thou dost desire all men to be saved and come to the knowledge of the truth, give quickening vigor to thy church, O God, that she may send forth men and women to the uttermost parts of the earth to witness to thy love in Christ Jesus and to the power of his Name. Grant unto thy people readiness to pray faithfully and to give generously toward the holy work whereunto thou hast called them, and impart to them strength that they weary not in well-doing.

Sow thy truth in the hearts of the people of this nation, that there may be a bounteous and perpetual harvest of peace and righteousness. To all who bear the sword of authority give the spirit of wisdom and understanding. Teach our people to provide things honest in the sight of all men, to give respect and obedience to the law, and to forsake the ways of darkness and the works of the flesh. Prosper all useful callings, all trustworthy service, and every wholesome enterprise. Bless our churches, schools, and institutions of mercy. Grant thy favor unto our homes so that our children may learn to walk in Christ, and our youth perceive that only godliness has the promise of the life that now is and of that which is to come.

With the healing dew of thy love refresh the spirits of all who are in affliction or danger of body or soul, and by thy grace uphold them in every trial. If any walk through the valley of the shadow of death, be thou the Companion of their way. Give unto the aged the eternal springtime of thy presence. Grant faith to him who is in doubt, and let him who is in the gall of bitterness taste of thy mercy.

These, and whatsoever other things according to thy pleasure we should have asked, vouchsafe unto us in the Name of our Lord and Savior, Jesus Christ. Amen.

APOSTLE

st. james the elder

July 25

O Lord God, heavenly Father, who, according to thine abundant mercy, hast begotten us again unto a living hope by the resurrection of Jesus Christ from the dead, we thank thee for the great love wherewith thou hast loved us, saving us by the cross of thy Son and bringing us from the dominion of sin and the power of death to a pure and indestructible heritage in the presence of thy glory.

We praise thee this day especially for the grace granted unto thy servant James the Elder, who, in the strength of a mighty faith, took up his cross and obediently followed the Lord Jesus and who, in his martyrdom, witnessed to a good confession. We bless thee for the manifestation in him that neither tribulation, nor distress, nor persecution, nor famine, nor nakedness, nor peril, nor sword, shall be able to separate us from the love of Christ. By the example of his unwavering spirit, instruct and quicken us, so that in the trials of our faith we may remain steadfast and true and attain unto the eternal kingdom whereunto thou hast appointed us.

For thy church and people we pray. Grant that they may never want for true pastors to teach, exhort, counsel, and warn them in wisdom and love. Stir up the power of godliness in our midst, that our profession may be sincere; and by thy might strengthen us in whatever conflict we must face. And as thy searching eye discerns the faithless, the impenitent, and the hypocritical, convert them so that thy church in no way may be weakened.

Bestow the light of thy truth upon the nations of the earth, that men may not fear them that can kill the body, but thee, O God, who art able to destroy both body and soul. Help them to realize thy presence in their national life and to walk before thee in lowly and loving reverence.

Set thy holy angels to watch over our land, that we may live in the peace of righteousness. Give us laws that conform to thy laws, citizens who obey the established ordinances, and civil servants who administer their offices with enlightened character and conscience, so that we may have domestic tranquility and concord. Root out from among us the love of pleasure, ease, and indolence; the worship of money, the imitation of corrupt idols, and the glorification of vain philosophies that destroy virtue, integrity, and personal dignity. Grant unto us the wholesome spirit of honesty, industry, and morality.

Look this day in compassion upon all the sick and the suffering, the aged and the infirm, the oppressed and the imperiled, the sorrowing and the dying, and hold them in thine everlasting arms. We pray that they may bear their affliction in the spirit of Christ, listen for the still, small voice of thy tender love, and trust in thee for help and victory.

And as thy Son, our Savior Jesus Christ, has declared that we must enter thy heavenly kingdom through much tribulation, we humbly entreat thee neither to leave us nor forsake us, and by thy Spirit to preserve us unto the coming in glory of him by whom thou wilt judge the world.

These petitions we bring unto thee with true hearts, confessing our sins and unworthiness, and asking all in the holy Name of thy Son Jesus. Amen.

APOSTLE

st. barcholomew

August 24

Lord God of hosts, whom no man can call upon unless he believes, nor believe in unless he has heard, nor hear unless the Word of thy truth has been preached unto him, we thank thee that thou didst provide disciples of honest and true heart, so that they, hearing the Word of Jesus Christ, beholding the things that were done by him, and being eyewitnesses of his Passion and glory, might in faith effectually preach the Gospel of thy salvation, edify thy people, and lay the foundation for thy church. We bless thee for their labors and self-denial, for their doctrine and obedience, for their suffering and tribulation, and for their endurance even unto their end.

We give thee praise this day especially for the calling of the blessed Apostle Bartholomew, who continued with Christ our Lord in all his temptations and who went forth with thy Word before the nations.

Grant unto us, O God, that we may be instructed in the wisdom which has been delivered unto us by the mouth of thy prophets and apostles and most perfectly revealed in the fullness of grace and truth in Jesus Christ. And, that we may be obedient thereto, open our hearts to the influence of thy Holy Spirit, that he may rule and govern our thoughts, words, and deeds. Turn us from our manifold sins and give us true repentance and faith, that we may walk sincerely and without guile before thee all the days of our life, and enter the joy of that salvation which thou hast prepared before the foundation of the world for all who confess and obey thine only-begotten Son Jesus Christ.

And as he is the Head of the church and the Shepherd of thy people, let them be strong in his might, increased in the knowledge of his saving love, and fruitful in every good work. To this end give them pastors and teachers who shall establish them firmly in the faith by Word and Sacrament, warn them lest they be spoiled through vain philosophy or deceit, and lead them to covet spiritual gifts earnestly.

Exalt thy Son before the nations of the earth, that they may behold and acknowledge him as the Way, the Truth, and the Life, and be delivered from thy righteous judgment. Look with thy favor upon our land, and by thy mercy preserve us from all who hate us. Let Christ and his cross be preached from shore to shore to the saving of multitudes who are now in darkness and in bondage to the flesh. Give us leaders who have thy law written in their hearts and a people who obey thy commandments. Defend our homes from the lusts of the flesh and the love of the world. Keep our children in the covenant of thy grace, and our parents in the bonds of charity.

Help all who are afflicted in body, mind, or spirit, or who are suffering any adversity or trial, to know the love of Christ which passes knowledge, and to be filled with all the fullness of thy mercy and peace; and grant that when they call upon thee in their necessity, thou wilt bestow upon them thy bounteous goodness.

And now, O Father, giving thanks unto thee always for all things, we entreat thee to vouchsafe unto us these and such other things as we have need of, in the Name of our Lord Jesus Christ, and for his sake. Amen.

st. matthew

September 21

Almighty God, our Father, who didst ordain thy Son Jesus, by the faithful obedience of his innocent sufferings and death, to receive the throne and kingdom of David, to order and establish it forever with righteousness and mercy, we thank thee that thou hast highly exalted him, making him Lord over all thy creation and Head over all thy church.

Grant unto us thy Holy Spirit, that we may be begotten again by faith into newness of life, walk perseveringly in all humility, repentance, and righteousness, and receive the inheritance in that eternal kingdom prepared for thy believing people from the foundation of the world.

For all thy servants who, by the inspiration of thy Spirit, have faithfully preserved unto us the record of our Lord's mission and ministry, his words and acts, his cross and resurrection, we give praise. Especially do we bless thy Name this day for the life and labors of the holy apostle and evangelist Matthew, who, called by thy Son to follow him and know the righteousness which is by faith, entered with readiness into the fellowship of Christ's sufferings and the joy of his salvation.

Vouchsafe unto us, O God, that through all the manifold changes and dangers of this life we may remain steadfast in the doctrines of our Lord and his apostles, and that thereby we may grow in the knowledge of him and of the things that pertain to his kingdom.

Suffer us never to be deceived or to fall into error, doubt, or unbelief.

Look in mercy upon the nations of the earth and, although many have deserved thy righteous wrath, withhold thy just punishments for the sake of those within their borders who call upon thy Name and who tremble at thy Word. Pour out upon them the dew of thy heavenly grace, that the wicked may turn from their way and live, and that thy people may be confirmed in thy judgment.

Turn our own nation into the straight paths of honesty, justice, and peace. Forgive her manifold sins and heal her of her transgressions. Endow all her magistrates with true wisdom and integrity, that we may be governed according to thy pleasure

Bless our churches and schools, all institutions of mercy, and all endeavors to raise the fallen, the homeless, the fatherless, the handicapped, the sick, and the wounded. Let our children be nourished by the words of faith and love and our people edified by divine truth. Raise up among us an increasing number whose wills are conformed to thy will, whose hearts and lives have been surrendered to the furtherance of thy kingdom at home and abroad, and who in obedience thereto fear no man.

Give wisdom to the perplexed and peace to the anxious; sustain and comfort all who are in any way afflicted. Wherever any may be hated for thy Name's sake, defend them by thy power and overthrow their persecutors. Deliver the oppressed from their misery, and grant hope and amendment to all who are imprisoned.

And as here we have no continuing abode, preserve us lest any root of bitterness rise up to destroy the hope of thy promise, and help us to attain to the heavenly mansions prepared for us by thy Son Jesus Christ, our Lord and Savior, in whose holy Name we pray. Amen.

st. michael

September 29

O Lord of hosts, King eternal, immortal, and invisible, the only wise God, we give thee honor and glory for the providence thou hast extended from the foundation of the world over all thy people through thy holy angels, who do always behold thy face, worship thy majesty and execute thy commandments.

Especially do we bless thee that thou didst abundantly manifest their presence throughout the earthly life of our Lord Jesus Christ, calling upon thy flaming messengers to reveal to the holy family thy glorious purposes, to fill the heavens with the songs of peace and good will at his birth, to strengthen him in his temptation and Passion, and to declare his resurrection and ascension to his disciples.

Grant, heavenly Father, that as thou hast appointed them to do thy will and to minister to those who shall be heirs of salvation, they may be given charge concerning us, so that we may be delivered from every peril that threatens us. Save us from the assaults of the devil, from the pride, vanities, and deceits of this wicked world, and from its love of the flesh, of place, and of power. Protect us against every calamity by storm or fire, war or accident, pestilence or famine, and in all tribulation uphold us by thy mercy. By thy Word give us light, we pray, for our earthly pilgrimage, so that we may repent of our sins, continue steadfast in faith, and persevere in every good work, and at the end be granted the crown of life which abides forever.

Shield thy church, O God, from the hands of all who hate her.

Send forth thine angels speedily to defend all who are persecuted and oppressed for thy Name's sake, to quench the violence of torture and to turn the edge of the sword. Grant the fullness of thy Holy Spirit to thy people, that they may accomplish with faith, courage, and obedience all that thou hast called them to do.

Be merciful unto the multitudes in every nation. And forasmuch as in thine own time thou wilt reveal thy Son Jesus from heaven with his mighty angels, to take flaming vengeance on them that have denied thee, blasphemed thy Name, and rejected thy love in Christ, grant unto the nations time for the conversion of their hearts and the amendment of their ways. To this end raise up pastors and missionaries who with boldness and grace shall penetrate the dominions of darkness with thy Gospel and bring many sons to glory.

Make thy countenance to shine upon our own land. Give us the love of truth and righteousness. Grant thy favor to all who bear authority over us. Prosper all schools and colleges as they bear witness to thee. Bless those who labor with mind or hand in such services as are necessary for us. Let the spirit of thanksgiving and brotherliness prevail everywhere.

Direct thy holy angels to minister to all who are in want, trouble, pain, sorrow, disappointment, anxiety, or any other adversity, and comfort them with thy power and grace.

Grant that thy presence may brighten our homes, that our children may learn thy tender love and holy will, and that our parents may walk in the counsels of thy Son.

Now unto him in whose Name we pray and who will return on the last day with his angels to gather the elect from the uttermost reaches of the earth, to him be glory in the church and praise forever. Amen.

EVANGELIST

st. luke

October 18

Almighty and eternal God, Creator of heaven and earth, who in thy providence hast chosen what the world calls folly to confound what it deems wise; and what it counts weak, to shame what it counts strong; and the things which are despised, to bring to naught the things that are, so that no flesh shall glory in thy presence: We thank thee that in the crucified Christ thou didst manifest thy wisdom and power and by him bring us to redemption, sanctification, and righteousness.

We bless thee for the knowledge of him which thou hast vouchsafed unto us in the Holy Scriptures and praise thee that thou didst inspire the holy evangelists to record all that our Lord taught and did in his earthly ministry, so that we might know the certainty of those things wherein thou wouldst instruct us.

We praise thee this day especially for the beloved physician Luke, whom thou didst call to faith in Christ, send forth to search out from eyewitnesses the testimonies of his truth, and ordain to present, for the edification of thy people, all the things pertaining to thy Son's life and the beginnings of thy church, which thou didst desire. Grant that we may so read therein that, taught by thy Holy Spirit, we may be rooted and built up in Christ, filled with a knowledge of his will, and established in the true faith of his holy Name.

Send forth the light of thy Word unto every land, people, and tribe, that the eyes of the blind and the ears of the deaf may be opened.

182

Build highways to the nations and open the doors thereto, that thy church may bring the Gospel of Jesus to multitudes. Guide those who are spiritually lame to faith, that they may walk, and let those who cannot speak sing of his mercy. Raise up among us pastors, missionaries, teachers, and other workers who will offer themselves to thee for service in thy harvest, and grant their labors thy blessing. Forgive the sins of thy church, her lack of faith, want of love, and poverty of vision. Pour out thy Spirit upon us, that we may be fervent in heart and steadfast in obedience to all that our Lord has commanded.

Let thy doctrine drop like refreshing rain upon our land, and as the showers that water the earth bring forth fruit, so may mercy, peace, justice, and truth everywhere grow as the harvest of thy Word.

Bless our homes and families and nourish the children of the church with the knowledge and understanding that proceeds from thee.

Give thy benediction to our schools, colleges, universities, and seminaries, and endow them with grace to teach effectually those things which are profitable both for this life and the life to come.

Aid every institution of mercy and every endeavor to heal. Support and sustain those who are serving therein. Grant thy help to the sick and those in any other adversity, so that they may find that joy and gladness which thou dost afford to all the ransomed in Christ.

Uphold us all, O God, with the right hand of thy righteousness, and ever strengthen and lead us, so that we may journey through this world in confident and trusting faith, and finally, when thou callest us, be received into the everlasting peace and joy of thine eternal kingdom, through Jesus Christ our Lord. Amen.

st. simon and st. jude

October 28

Lord God, heavenly Father, who in ancient days didst speak unto our forefathers by thy prophets but who in the fullness of time didst speak unto us by thy Son Jesus Christ, we thank thee for the revelation of thyself in him and that thou didst make him thy true and living Word.

We give unto thee our heartfelt praise also, O Father, that thou hast spoken unto us by thy holy apostles, whom thou didst choose and instruct through thy Son in all the things which thou didst command thy people to believe and do; and that thou didst set them over thy church as thy faithful servants and thy Son's true witnesses.

And as they entered into Christ's temptations and loved not their lives unto death, grant that we may faithfully receive their testimony of all that they beheld, touched, and heard of the Word of Life, that by his grace we may be cleansed of all sin and receive the gift of everlasting life.

We give thee special thanks this day in remembrance of our fathers in Christ, Simon and Jude—of their labors and sacrifice, of their anointing, as it were for death, and of their being numbered among those who were persecuted, reviled, and defamed, yet who blessed and murmured not. Give us, we beseech thee, such unwavering faith and steadfast obedience to thy Word and will that we may be built up as living stones into a holy temple where thy Spirit may abide forever and where spiritual sacrifices, acceptable to thee in thy Son, are offered for the salvation of our souls.

Graciously bestow thy blessing upon thy church everywhere. Call forth from our midst young men and women of godly fear who will offer themselves for service in thy kingdom, and help us all to give freely of ourselves for thy work, even as we have freely received thy bountiful mercies.

Pour out thy Spirit upon the nations of the earth, that the lust for power, greed for gold, and love of the praise of men may be thwarted, and that in the knowledge and love of thee multitudes may turn to the truth and righteousness of our Lord Jesus.

Fill our land with the radiance of his love and life. Take from our midst all the hidden things of darkness and corruption, and prosper and defend all who labor for godliness and morality.

Establish the presence of our Lord Jesus Christ in our homes, that the little ones may learn from their parents to know and love him.

In thy compassion remember the sick and the sorrowing, the weary and the heavy-laden, the desolate and the defeated, the anxious and the perplexed, the weak and those that are bowed down in years, the despairing and the disappointed, the imperiled and those who unknowingly are facing great trials, and show them that in Christ the bruised reed shall not be broken and the smoking flax shall not be quenched.

Now, O Lord, we lay these petitions humbly and trustingly before thee, and pray that thou wouldst grant them unto us for the sake of thy well-beloved Son, Jesus Christ our Lord, in whose merits and righteousness alone we trust. Amen.

reformation day

October 31

Lord God of hosts, who through thy Holy Spirit didst call thy people by the Gospel of our Lord Jesus Christ and gather them into the fellowship of his Name, accept our humble and earnest thanks for thy continual watchfulness over thy church: defending her from the assaults of her ancient adversary, the devil, and from all the enemies of thy Word and will; delivering her from the error of false prophets and from the corruption of evil shepherds; and rescuing her during times of persecution, peril, and oppression.

Lord of our life, we praise thee this day especially that when thy church by reason of sin was taken in bondage to the words and works of men and when her light had fallen low thou didst in thy mercy revive her by raising up mighty men, chosen and ordained of thee, full of the Holy Ghost, faith, and wisdom, to lead thy people to the fountains of living truth, to restore to them the joy of thy salvation through the riches of thy grace, and to bring them through the righteousness which is by faith in thy Son Jesus to the adoption of sons and to the inheritance incorruptible.

Grant unto us, O God of our salvation, that, being justified freely by thine only-begotten Son, we may ever trust in thy loving-kindness, know the fullness of thy forgiveness for all our sins, and live in the Spirit unto all godliness, faith, love, and hope. And as the entrance of thy Word gives light, implant it in our hearts, that we, enlightened and sanctified thereby, may bring forth fruit by patient continuance in well-doing.

Lord of the living harvest, send forth laborers into thy harvest to proclaim thy Word to the nations and to gather from the four corners of the earth all who confess the power of Jesus' Name. Save thy church from heresy and schism, from lukewarmness and ease, and vouchsafe unto her vision, faithfulness, and zeal, that she may not come under thy judgment.

Father of mercies, look in mercy upon our land. Forgive us our trespasses, injustices, and lack of brotherhood. Endow those who hold authority of state with such love of truth, grace of mind, and purity of heart as will make them worthy to bear office and to receive thy favor. Let thy light shine forth in every city and town, that men everywhere may come to know thee and turn to thee in repentance and faith.

God of all comfort, we commend to thy loving care our homes and families. Where there is sin, create clean hearts; where there is grief and sorrow, grant the consolation of thy love; where there is trouble, bring the healing of thy love; where there is temptation and trial, instill a love of righteousness and godly trust; where there is fear, bestow the courage of thy presence; and where there is pain, impart strength and wholeness. Be thou the Refuge, the Solace, and the Shield of all, and to all a very present Help in trouble.

Eternal Father, strong to save, pour out thy Spirit upon us, that we may believe with our hearts in thy beloved Son, trust in him and his merits, walk in loving obedience to him, and finally be received in righteousness, innocence, and purity into thine eternal presence to dwell with thee and all thy people forever and ever. This we pray in the Name of our Lord Jesus Christ. Amen.

all saints' day

November 1

Almighty and ever-living God, who hast given light for the righteous and joy for the upright in heart, we praise thee for the precious
gift of thy Son Jesus Christ, our Lord, that thou hast saved us in him,
and through him hast called us with a holy calling according to thine
own purpose into fellowship with all thy saints and to an inheritance
incorruptible and undefiled, that fadeth not away.

We thank thee for thy church and that thou hast granted unto her
the glory of thine abiding presence, the power and truth of thy Holy
Spirit, and the communion of her Savior Jesus Christ. Keep her steadfast in thy Word and Sacraments, faithful to thy revelation and
obedient to the command of thy Son to proclaim thy Gospel to the
uttermost parts of the earth. May she hold forth the Word of Life
with zeal and fervor, so that multitudes out of every nation and kindred and people and tongue may sing of thy salvation and rejoice in
thy mercy. Endow thy people with the mind of the Spirit, that they
may possess the undaunted faith of the prophets, continue in the sound
doctrine of the apostles, and serve thee with the love and courage of
the martyrs. Help them so to live in the righteousness of Christ and
in obedience to his commandments that they may shine forth as
lights in this world and in thine eternal kingdom.

Raise up in thy church faithful shepherds who will diligently feed
the flock which Christ purchased with his own blood, and show
themselves in all things a pattern of good works. Preserve thy people

from heresy and schism, from the form of godliness rather than the power of it, from love of the world and the pride of life, from oppression and corruption, from enemies of the truth and lovers of wickedness, from persecutors and men of violence, from the devil, and from their own flesh. By thy Word so strengthen them in their pilgrimage through this world, that they may be brought at last safely to their heavenly home.

Vouchsafe therefore unto us, O Lord, such trust in Christ for our redemption that we may, with all who have died in him, receive at last the crown of life, inhabit the mansions he has gone to prepare for us, and come to those unspeakable joys which the mind of man cannot imagine nor the tongue of man describe.

Comfort the aged and the infirm with the blessed hope of thy heavenly rest; strengthen the weary and the burdened by the grace of Christ; give the spirit of power, love, and a sound mind to the fearful; heal the sick and the wounded by engrafting in them a true faith in thy holy Name; restore the sin-laden and conscience-stricken by the redeeming grace of the cross; set thy holy angels to watch over the imperiled and be the companion of the lonely; and console the sorrowing and the bereaved by the promise of the resurrection.

O Lord and Father, deliver us all from every evil of body or soul, and at last translate us from the Church Militant in this world of much striving and sadness to the Church Triumphant, to dwell in life and joy with thee and all thy children whom thou hast chosen in Christ Jesus before the foundation of the world.

These petitions we pray in his Name who is the Head of the church in heaven and on earth, even Jesus Christ our Redeemer. Amen.

the festival of harvest

O God, our Father, who hast created and upholdest all things in heaven and earth by the Word of thy power, who art good to all, and whose tender mercies are over all thy works: We enter thy gates of prayer with thanksgiving, and thy courts with praise. We praise thee for the blessings thou hast laid up for them that fear thee and wrought for them that trust in thee. We give thee our most humble and earnest thanks that thou didst stretch forth the hand of thy benediction upon the land at seedtime, that thou didst send forth thy Spirit and didst renew the face of the earth with the sunlight and the rain, the day's warmth and the evening dew, and hast clothed the earth with the garment of harvest.

Grant that we may ever be mindful of thy manifold goodness, O Lord: That thou hast brought us into a land flowing with milk and honey, rich in forest and abundant with pasture; a land with the strength of the hills and the treasures of the deep places of the earth, with fruitful seasons and mighty waters. Thou hast made our cup to run over; thou hast filled the horn of our plenty; thou hast prepared a table for us; thou hast opened the windows of heaven and poured out thy blessings. O God, we thank thee for these testimonies of thy loving-kindness.

And forasmuch as man cannot live by bread alone, we thank thee for the surpassing goodness of the sublime revelation of thyself in thy Word, for the knowledge it unfolds to us of thine infinite power and glory, for the wisdom it imparts to us in thy pure commandments and life-giving precepts, and for the light it provides for us to discern thine eternal will and grace. Implant within us this holy seed, that we may bring forth the fruits of godliness in faith, mercy, and purity. Show us that life is more than meat, and the body than raiment.

But most especially do we thank thee for the unspeakable love and mercy thou didst bestow upon us in sending thine only-begotten Son Jesus Christ to deliver us by his cross from the bondage of sin, death, and the devil, and to secure for us by his resurrection the sure promise and living hope of eternal life.

Deliver us from every temptation and the trust in uncertain riches. Teach us to use wisely all that thou hast granted unto us and that thou wilt call us into account for our stewardship. Give us a vision of the needs of mankind for the light of the Gospel and compassion for all who are in want.

Grant thy blessing to all the afflicted, especially to those who are suffering for thy Name's sake. Give them the assurance that thine eyes are on the righteous and thine ears are open unto their prayers, and vouchsafe unto them a happy issue out of all their trials.

Let thy counsel prevail amongst the nations of the earth, and teach them to do thy will. Endow our land with the spirit of true religion and brotherhood; prosper uprightness in every office in government and society, and hinder every unwise and unwholesome endeavor. Open thy hand and satisfy the spiritual needs of our families with thy truth and love, that they may find the joy of thy grace in the possession of pure hearts, right motives, high resolves, self-discipline, and steadfast faith.

These petitions we offer unto thee, Lord God, holy Father, in the Name of thy dear Son, to whom be honor and glory forever. Amen.

A DAY OF
humiliation and prayer

O Lord God almighty, who didst stretch forth the heavens and lay the foundations of the earth, and in whose hand are the life, breath, and being of all things, we humble ourselves before thine infinite power and beseech thine invincible aid. Be thou our Refuge and Strength, a very present help in trouble. Gird on the sword of thy might and deliver us speedily, that thy Name may be praised in all generations and that thy truth may be served forever and ever.

O holy and righteous Lord, who lovest goodness and hatest iniquity, we confess that we have sinned against thee and thy will in thought, word, and deed; that we have transgressed thy law and commandments and done evil in thy sight; that we have rebelled against the authority of thy Word and gone after our own way; and that we have professed thee with our lips, but our hearts have been far from thee. We acknowledge that in our blindness and wickedness we have neither feared nor loved nor trusted thee. We repent most earnestly and sincerely, O God, with weeping and mourning, that we have offended against thy holy majesty and are altogether unclean.

O Father of mercies and God of all comfort, we turn by thy grace from our sins and plead that thou wilt forgive us for the sake of thy dear Son, Jesus Christ our Lord. By the blood of his cross cleanse us from all unrighteousness and spare us from the just recompense and reward of our iniquity. Blot out in thy great love the handwriting of ordinances against us, forgive the thoughts of our hearts, and prepare

192

our souls for the indwelling of thy Holy Spirit, that we may no more walk after the flesh, but ever seek the way of uprightness in mind and obedience in heart. Be merciful unto us and save us from the evil which threatens us, that we may rejoice in thy salvation and glorify thy Name.

And as thou resistest the proud, but givest grace to the humble, and as thou puttest down the mighty and the vain, but exaltest those who are meek and lowly, give us the Spirit of thy Son Jesus, that in lowliness of heart we may walk before thee all the days of our life, fearing none but thee, loving none above thee, trusting none more than thee.

Arm us, O Father, with every spiritual weapon, that we may resist the wiles of the devil, fight the good fight of faith, and lay hold of eternal life. When a cross is laid upon us, suffer us not to be tempted above that we are able, and show us the way to deliverance. Uphold us in our trials, that we neither falter nor waver in the faith, nor doubt or despair of thy power, but that, as thou knowest how to deliver the godly out of temptation, we may in patience, meekness, and trust leave all things in thy saving hand.

Teach us in this hour, dear God, to learn that we are ever dependent upon thee, and correct us so that we may walk in a straight path. Show us thy love in our need, and grant that as we love thee with all our hearts, minds, and strength, all things may work together for our good.

All these things we pray, O Lord, entreating thee in the Name of thine only-begotten Son, Jesus Christ our Savior, and in the faith of his promise that whatsoever we ask of thee in his Name thou wilt grant. Amen.

CONGREGATION

anniversary

O God, our Refuge and Fortress, who in Christ hast brought us into thy household, the church, and made us fellow citizens with the saints, fill us with loving gratitude and praise for every grace and gift thou hast bestowed upon us and upon all thy people from generation to generation.

For the courage of the prophets we thank thee. Give us in thy church in this day a like spirit of loyalty and heroic zeal. For the testimony of the apostles we give thee glory. Help us to continue steadfast in their doctrine and example. For the witness of all the martyrs we sing thy praise. Teach us also, O God, to take up our cross daily and follow our Savior with unfaltering steps. For the truth of the Reformers we give thanks to thee. Grant us by thy mercy to have the same spirit of wisdom and understanding in the things that pertain to our eternal salvation. For those who brought the light of thy truth to this land we thank thee. Help thy church today to hold aloft the light of life, that all men may come to know thy love in Jesus Christ.

We give thee praise, O Father, for the faith and testimony of those who have gone before us in the history of our congregation. Of thy glory, they have told us. Of thy goodness, they have shown us. Of thy love, they have spoken to us. A godly heritage have they bestowed upon their children and upon all their successors-in-the-faith in this place. Thou didst preserve them in faith and life. Preserve us, O God, by

194

thy mercy. Thou didst keep them in the unity of the Spirit and the bonds of peace. So keep us. Thou didst uphold them in many labors and defend them in many trials. So uphold and defend us. Thou didst extend loving-kindness to them in their failures and weaknesses. Even so, forgive us, O God of our fathers.

And now we pray that thou wouldst help this thy church ever to stand firmly upon the foundation of the apostles and the prophets, Jesus Christ himself being the chief cornerstone. Build us together into a holy temple for a habitation of the Spirit. Help us by word and deed, by true faith, living hope, and loving service to show forth thy glory and praise and to proclaim the unsearchable riches of Christ.

We pray for all members of this congregation in distant places, our young men and women still on this continent and those in far away lands. As thou didst deliver our fathers in perils of land and sea, deliver these of our brethren from all dangers, and stretch forth over them the right hand of thy power. Lead them in safety, and in thine own good time bring them again to their homes. Be present with our students preparing for the ministry and our deaconesses-in-training. Cause our church's schools and all Christian education to prosper, and bless our church's societies in the work to which they have committed themselves for Christ's sake. Especially we ask thee to bestow thy mercy and strength on the sick, the suffering, the sorrowing, and the lonely. Be with us all, renew our faith, inspire in us obedience, forgive our sins, and hear our prayers. For the sake of Jesus Christ, our one Lord, through whom we are bound into one body, with one faith, and possessing one sure and certain hope—eternal life in him. Amen.

the home

O thou God of all men, who hast been our dwelling place in all generations, and under whose shadow we abide, who wouldst encourage us to believe that thou art truly our Father and that we are thy children indeed, hear now our prayer.

We thank thee for the homes where Christ's spirit dwells, where true love reigns, and where loving service one of the other is practiced. We praise thee for the homes that are sanctified by the daily toil, courage, and sacrifice of godly parents, and that are blessed by a readiness to understand, a willingness to forgive, and an eagerness to help. We thank thee for all the goodness and joy in our homes today, for all the cherished and tender memories of our parents and homes in days now long past, and for all the bright promise of new homes and new families.

Be thou, O God, the protecting hand to guard our families from every peril and pitfall, to shield them from strife and discord, to defend them in trial and temptation. At each hearth overcome all suspicion and selfishness, all pride and misunderstanding. Lead thy people to seek for their homes neither wealth nor luxury, but the eternal, fathomless riches of Christ. Give us good and true parents who will honor their baptismal vows, suffer their little ones to come unto Jesus, and rear them in the nurture and admonition of the Lord.

Teach us, we pray, the sanctity of the home and the sacredness of the bond of marriage. Grant all parents and children grace to live together according to thy Word; strengthen husbands and wives in constant fidelity, and let them grow in true affection toward one another; sustain and defend our families in every peril of body or soul and give thy holy angels charge concerning them. To each husband and wife, each father and mother, each son and daughter present before thee this day, give a special measure of thy grace, that in Jesus Christ they may build happier, purer, stronger homes. Establish them in the truth of Christ's redeeming power and love, so that they may be able to endure the strain, the storm, and trouble of this turbulent world and remain immovable and unshakeable in the saving grace of his Word and promise.

Bless the sick and suffering, the sorrowing and grief-stricken both here and elsewhere; help them to remember that whom the Lord loves, he chastens. Grant that all who endure the fires of affliction may be brought to stronger faith, greater hope, and wider love.

Help us all to pass through this world in faith toward thee, in communion with thy holy church, and in loving service one of the other, that we may enjoy thy heavenly benediction and finally dwell in thy house forever. We ask all this in the Name and for the sake of Jesus Christ. Amen.

A DAY OF

thanksgiving

O Lord, heavenly Father, who from everlasting to everlasting art God, and who hast been our dwelling place in all generations: We give thanks unto thee that from the beginning of the world thou hast shown forth thy loving-kindness every morning and thy faithfulness every night.

We praise thee for the glorious gift of thy beloved Son, Jesus Christ our Lord, the faithful Witness of thy grace and mercy and the Ransom to redeem us from all our iniquity, whom thou didst raise as the First-begotten of the dead, that he might bring many sons to glory. Grant that by faith in him we may be clothed in his righteousness and made heirs of eternal life.

We thank thee for the Holy Scriptures, which thou didst give through the inspiration of thy Spirit, that in the knowledge of thy Word and will, and in the understanding of thy commandments and testimonies, we might have light for our way and truth for our shield. Give thy Word entrance into our lives, and let it rule the thoughts of our hearts.

We bless thee for the gift of the Holy Ghost, whom thou didst pour out upon thy people to instruct them in thy wisdom, lead them into thy obedience, warn them against sin, deliver them from evil, and prepare them for judgment. Grant that he may dwell within us and impart to us his manifold spiritual gifts.

We extol thy glory for calling, gathering, enlightening, and preserving thy church in every age; for her obedience to the commandments of her Lord and continuance in the doctrine of the apostles; for her prayers and sacrifices; for her devotion and service; and for her fellowship with her Lord and with multitudes out of every nation whom he has knit together in faith and love in one body. Preserve us in her holy communion.

We acknowledge with humble gratitude to thee the blessings that are ours in this goodly land: its heritage of freedom with responsibility, education with truth, individual worth with integrity, law with justice, and brotherhood with honor. For the labors and sacrifices of all who have given of themselves for the preservation and maintenance of these virtues, we thank thee.

For the beauties and endowments of our country, its bright valleys and majestic mountains, the riches of its mines and the goodness of its soil, its cattle on a thousand hills, its fruitful plains and abundant pastures, its homes and its industries, its schools and its libraries, and for all the many useful arts, sciences, and labors, we praise and thank thee.

For the wisdom thou hast granted our statesmen, for the integrity of just men in high office, for the diligence of every faithful public servant, for the strength and courage of our spiritual watchmen and counselors, for the knowledge and skill of the men of medicine and healing, for the incorruptibility of those who defend our laws, and for the heroism and selflessness of the multitudes who have guarded us and still stand watch upon the ramparts, we bow in gratitude before thee. O God, how great, how good, how wise, how loving thou art.

Be thou ever our Refuge and Fortress. Without thee we are as nothing. Thou hast done all, and thou hast given all without any merit or worthiness in us. We acknowledge our transgressions and humble ourselves before the throne of thy mercy. Forgive us our sins. Turn us from the ways of darkness. Absolve us, O Lord, and make us whole through faith in Jesus Christ our Lord.

Let thine eye be over thy church; save it from faithlessness and weakness and purify it by thy Spirit, that it may be strong in thy holy service.

Stretch forth the right hand of thy power and deliver our country from corruption and wickedness, that it may live in quietness and peace.

Send the light of thy love into all homes, that they may be nourished by the truth and grace of Jesus Christ and find joy in his presence.

Uphold the weak and the afflicted; let the health of thy grace flood their spirits. Protect those who are in danger of body or soul, and defend the persecuted and oppressed; let thy holy angels have charge concerning them.

Save us, Lord of hosts, lest we forget that the sum of all our good and the source of all our blessing are in thee and thee only, and that thou rewardest them who sincerely love and diligently seek thee.

Now unto him that loved us and washed us in his own blood and made us kings and priests unto thee, O Father, and in whose Name we pray, even Jesus Christ thy Son, to him be glory and dominion forever and ever. Amen.